This Coloring book
Belongs to

_____

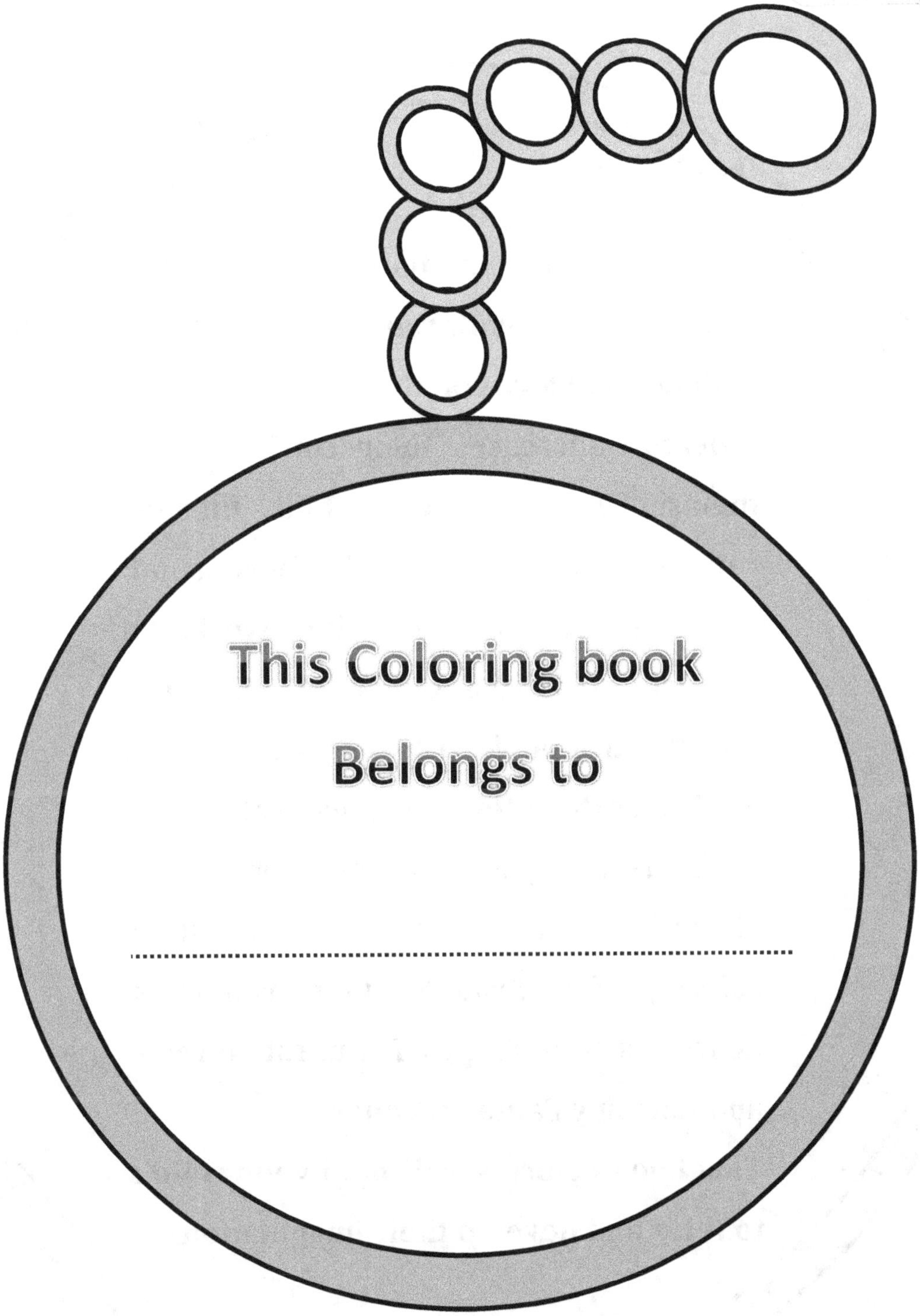

The coloring activity raises the imagination of children and gives them patience and focus on details.

Where it increases their confidence in themselves, when the child finishes completing a piece of art, he feels proud, and some may display his best works on the walls of his own room to brag about.

We offer this book with attractive content For lovers the interesting, magical lives!

In this coloring book, we present various Magical Unicorns pictures to enjoy their coloring, fly through stars, rainbows, hearts, various shapes, Beautiful Flowers, and Relaxing Fantasy Scenes

This book coloring will help your child's to relax and develop their imagination.

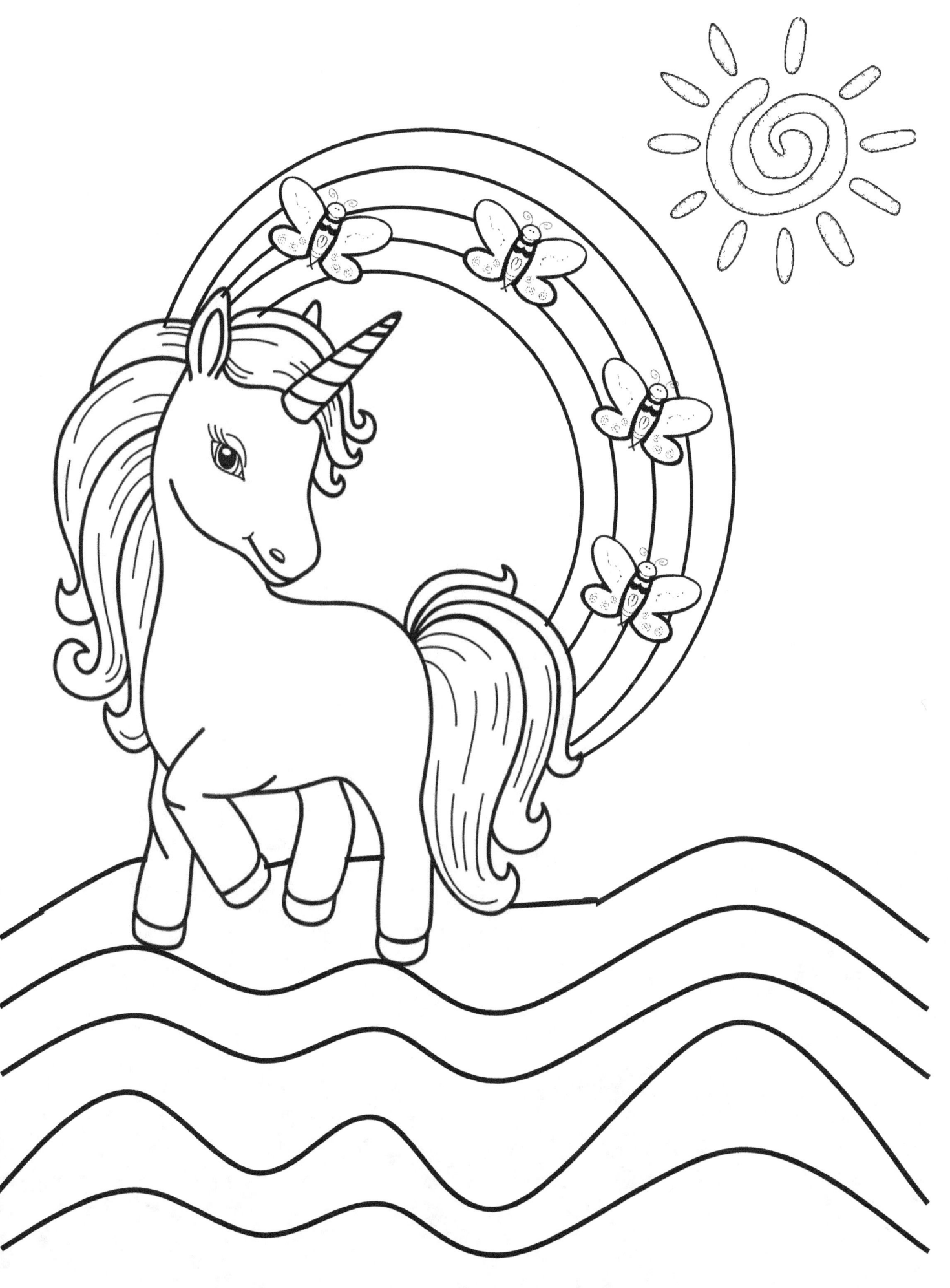

UNICORN

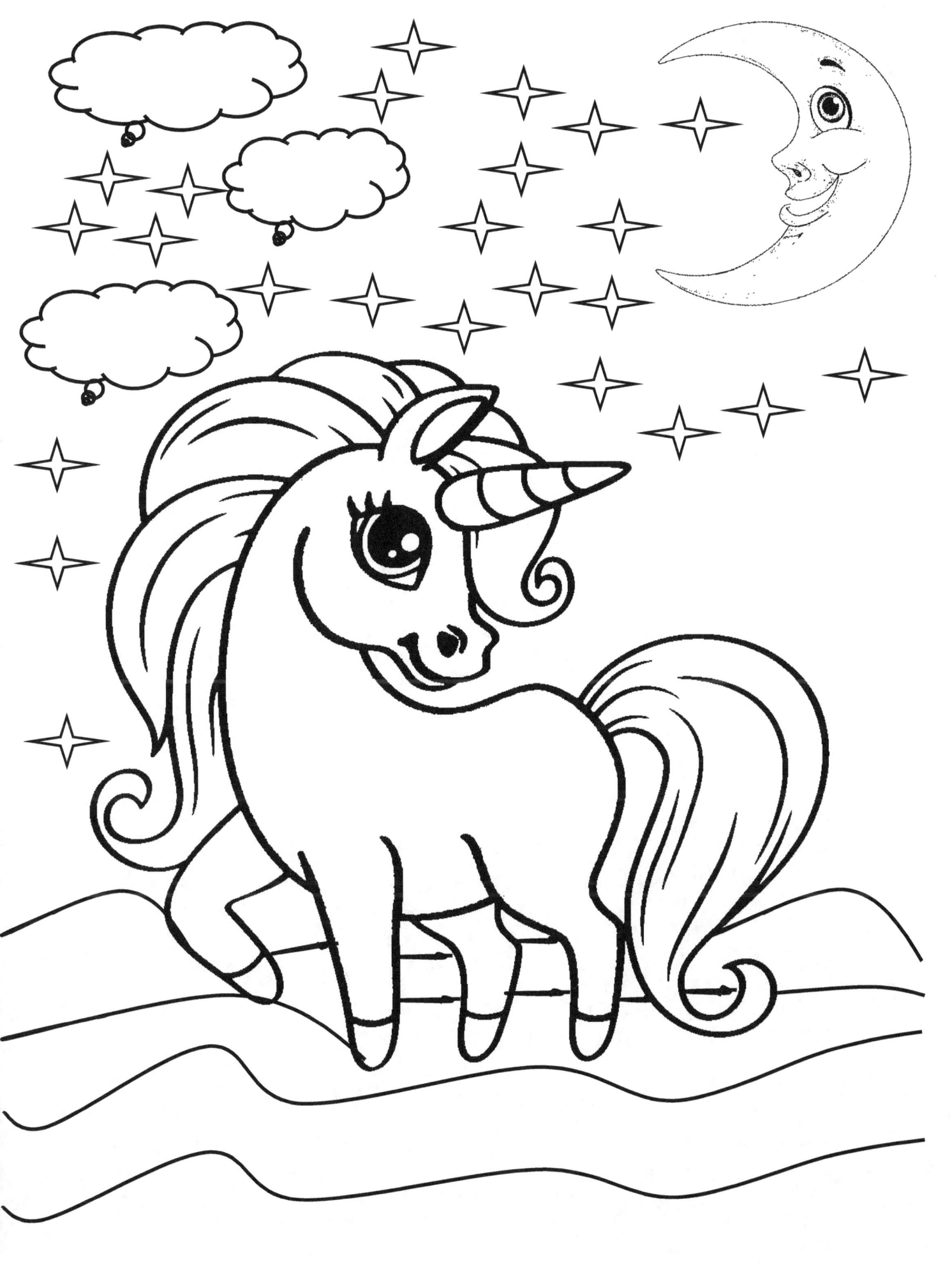

UNICORN

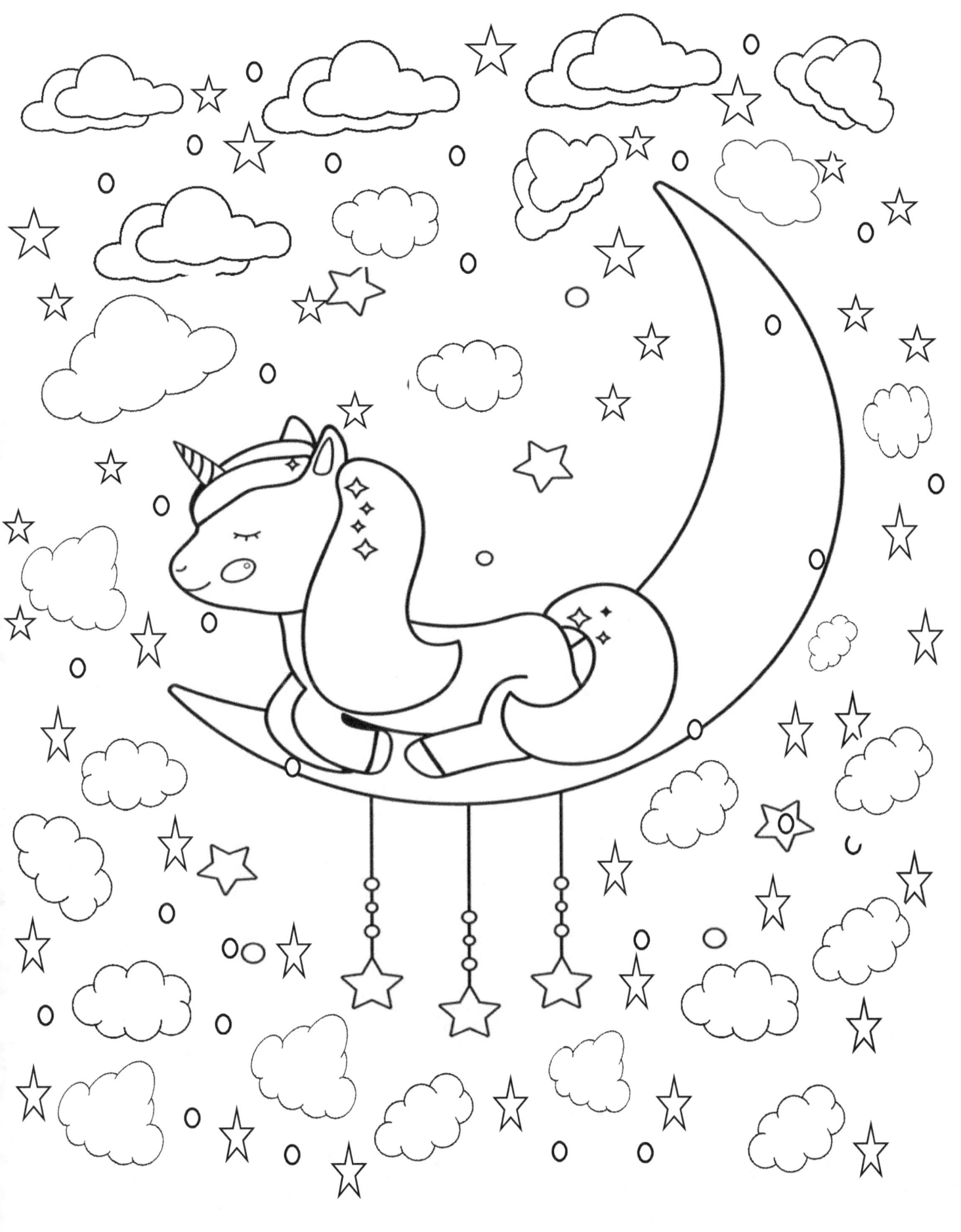

UNICORN

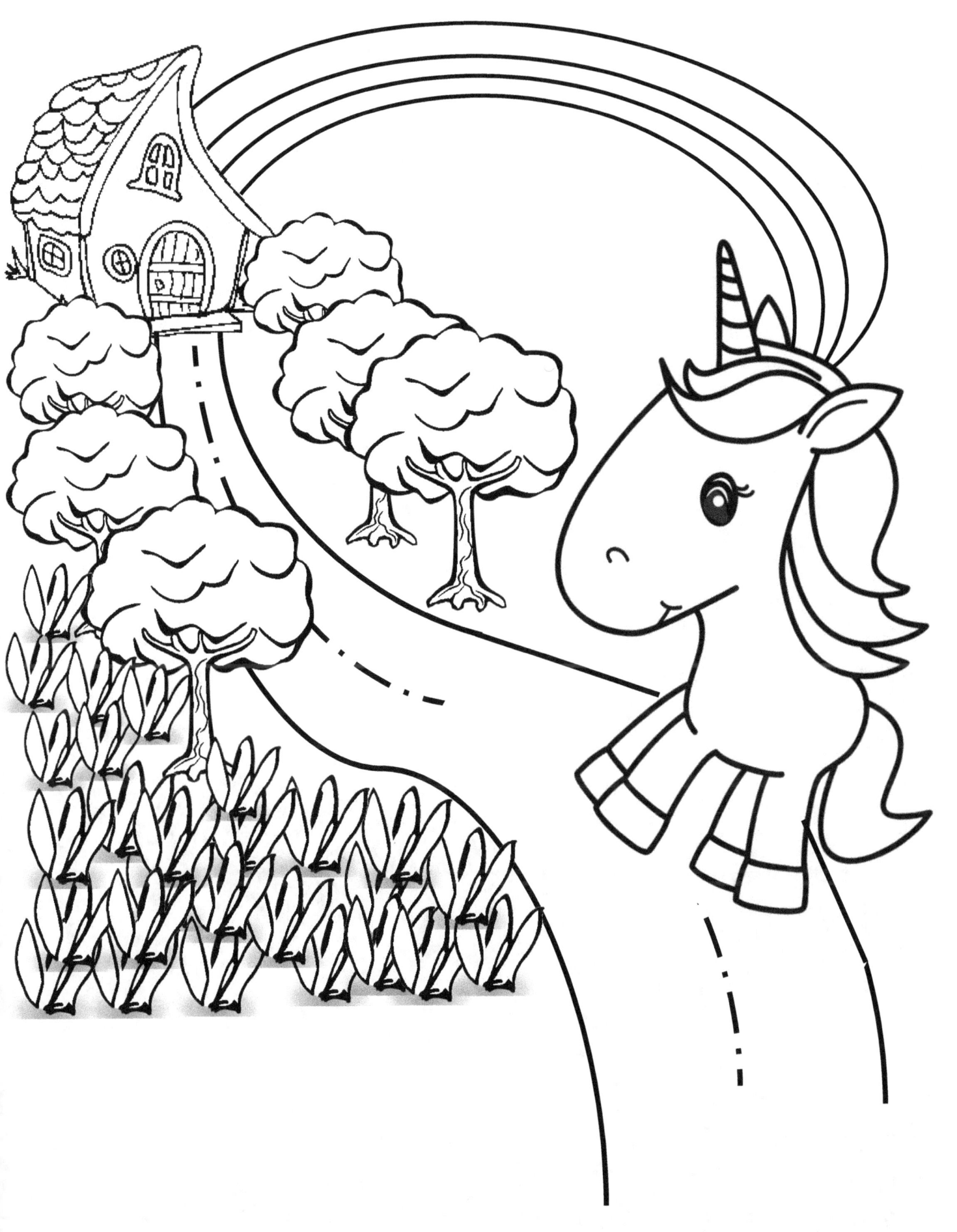

UNICORN

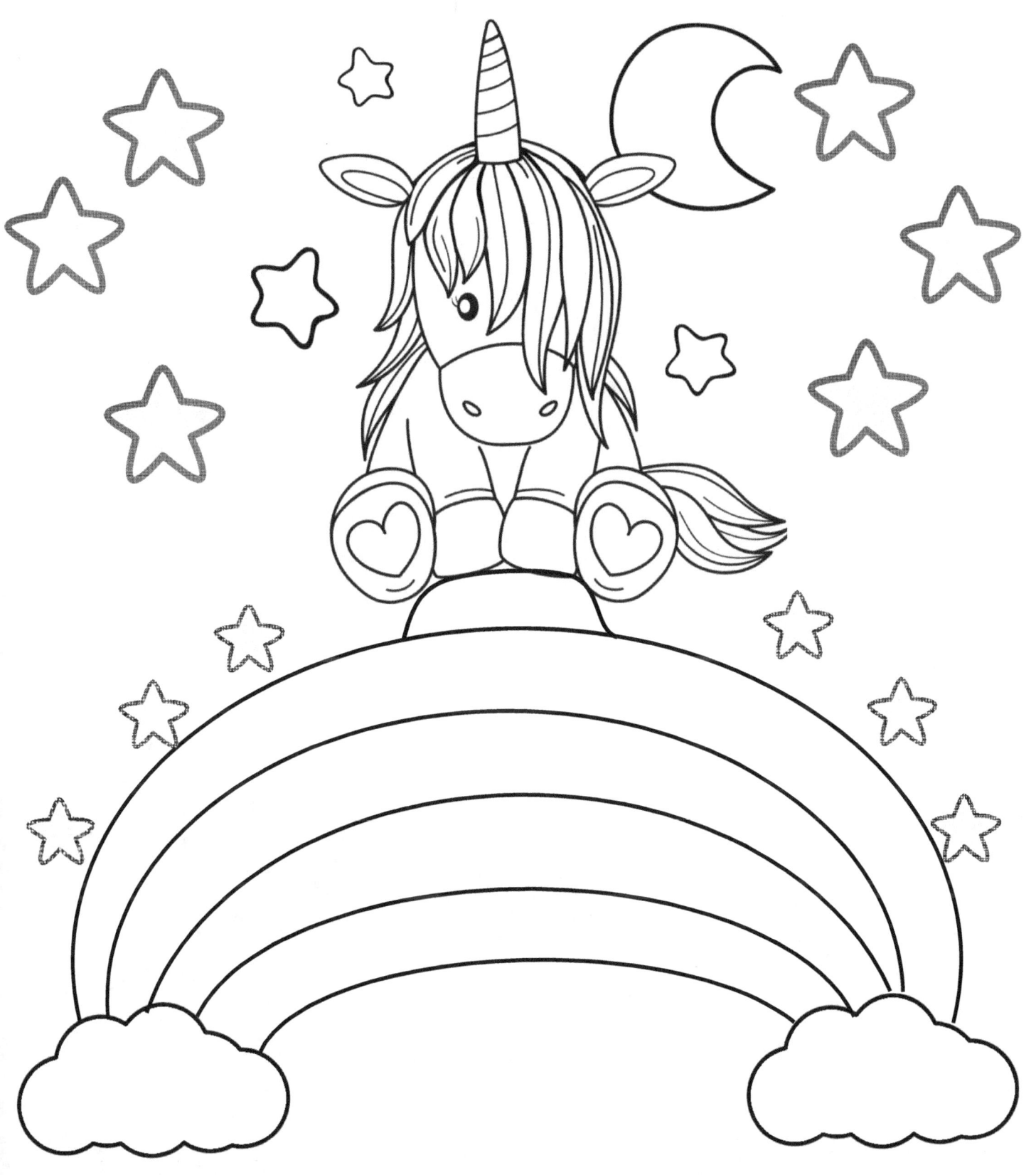

UNICORN

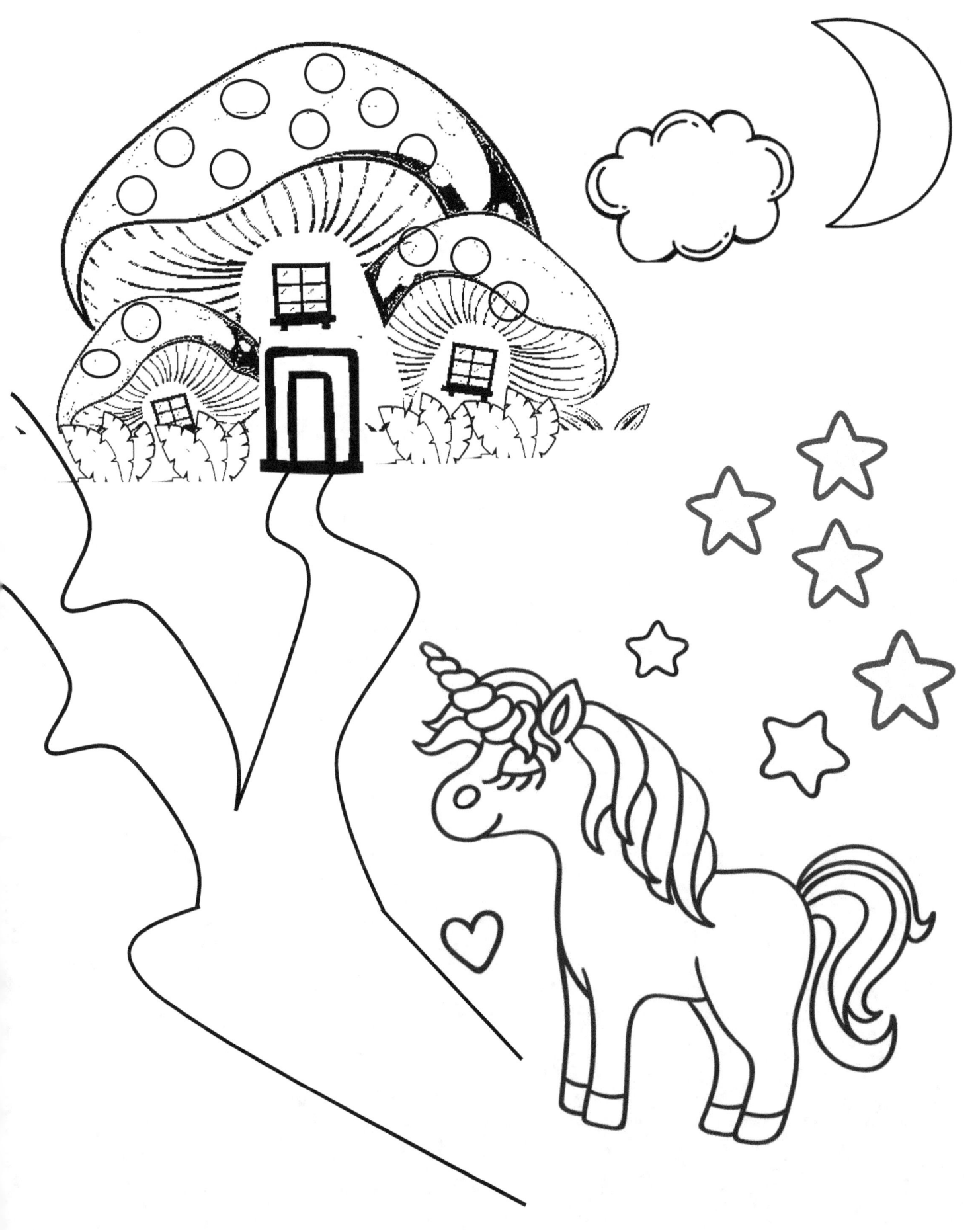

UNICORN

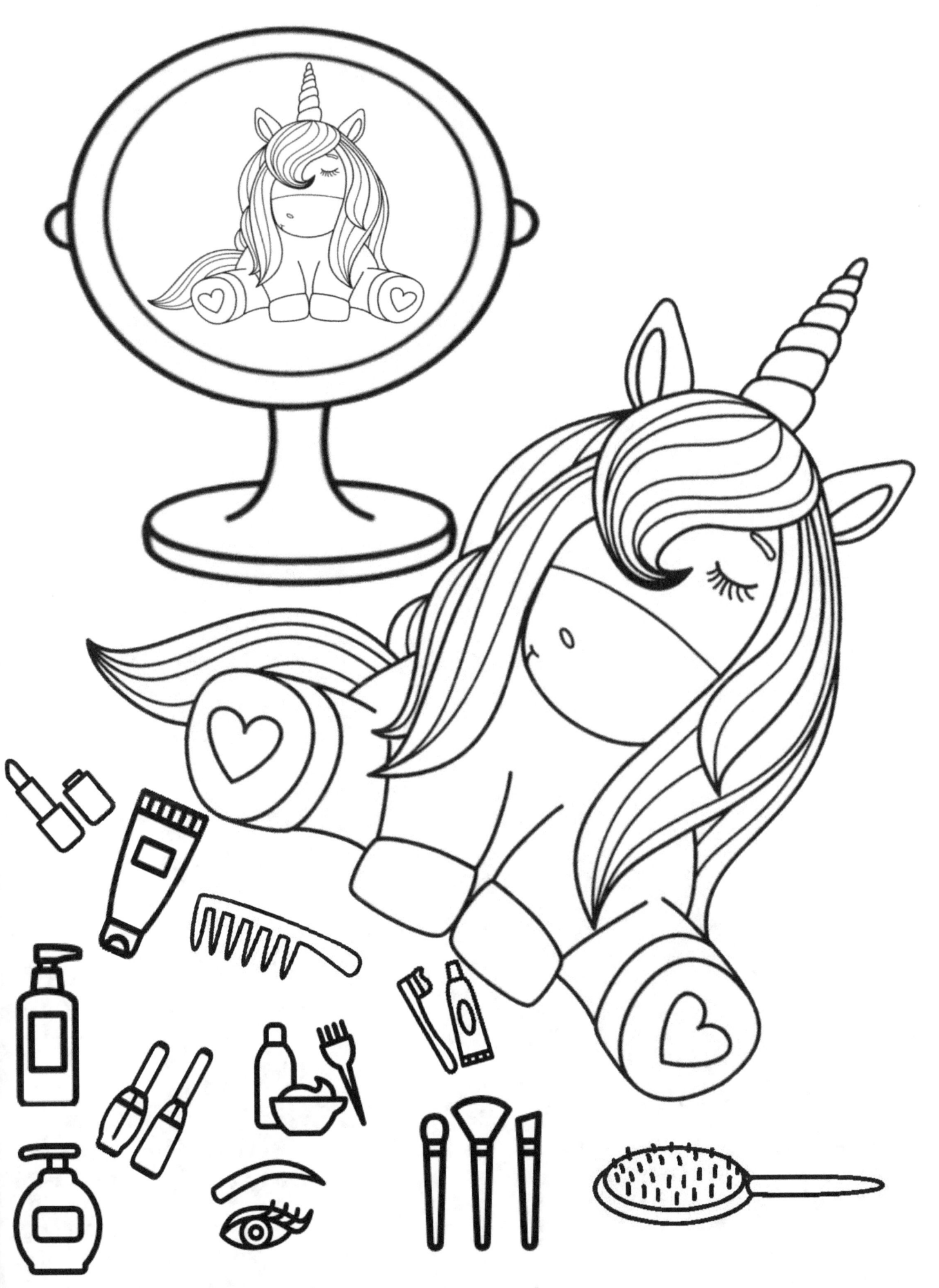

UNICORN

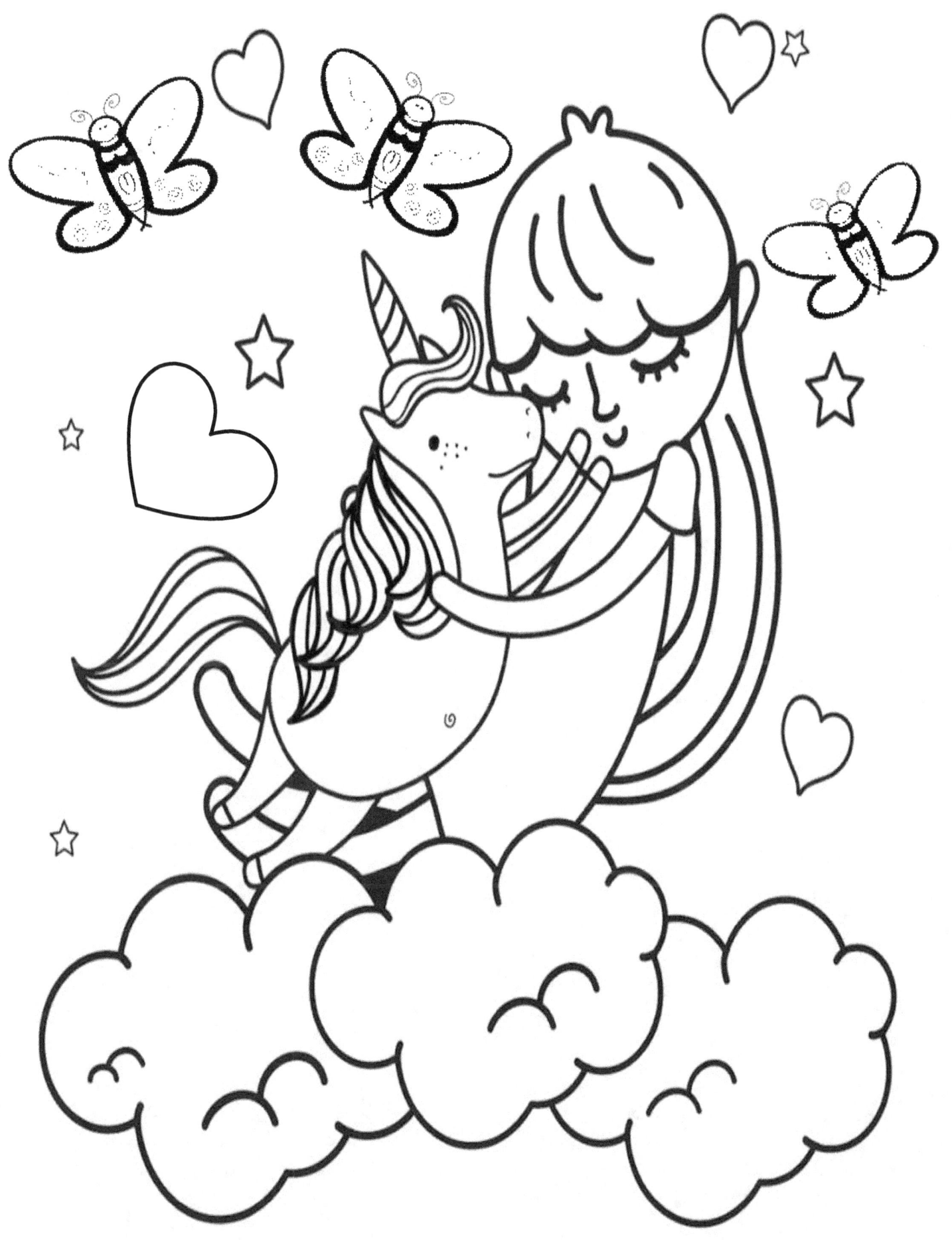

UNICORN

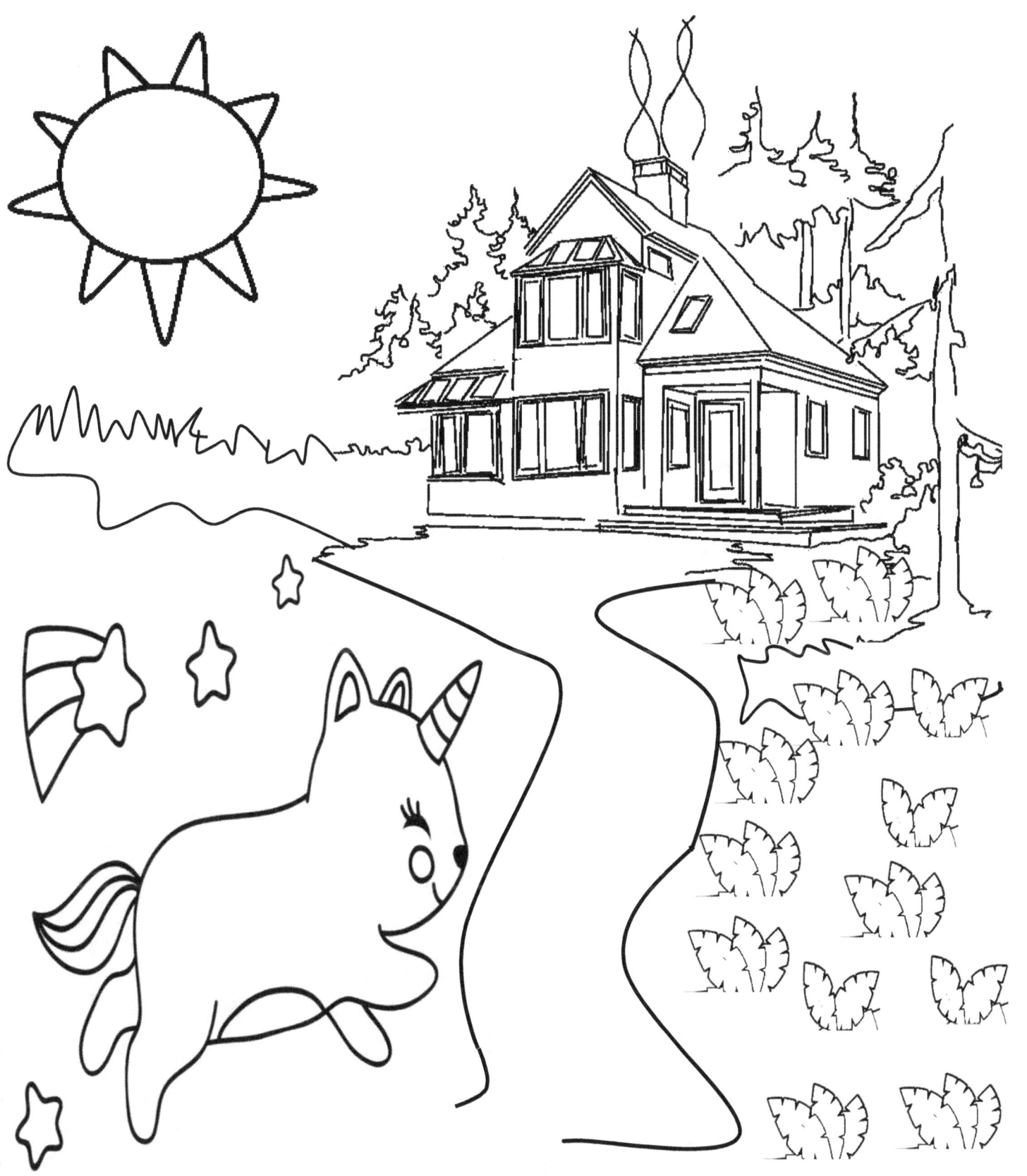

UNICORN

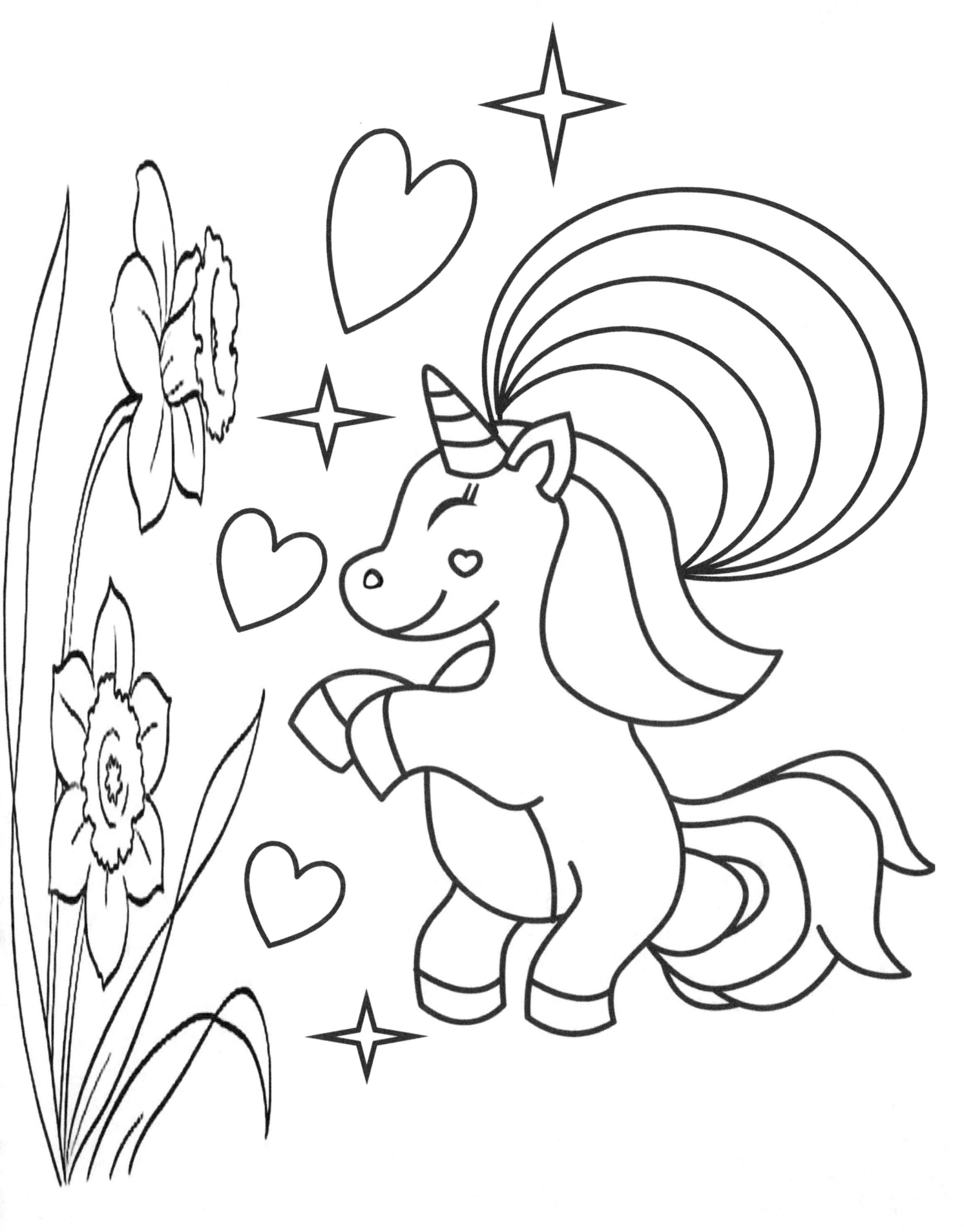

UNICORN

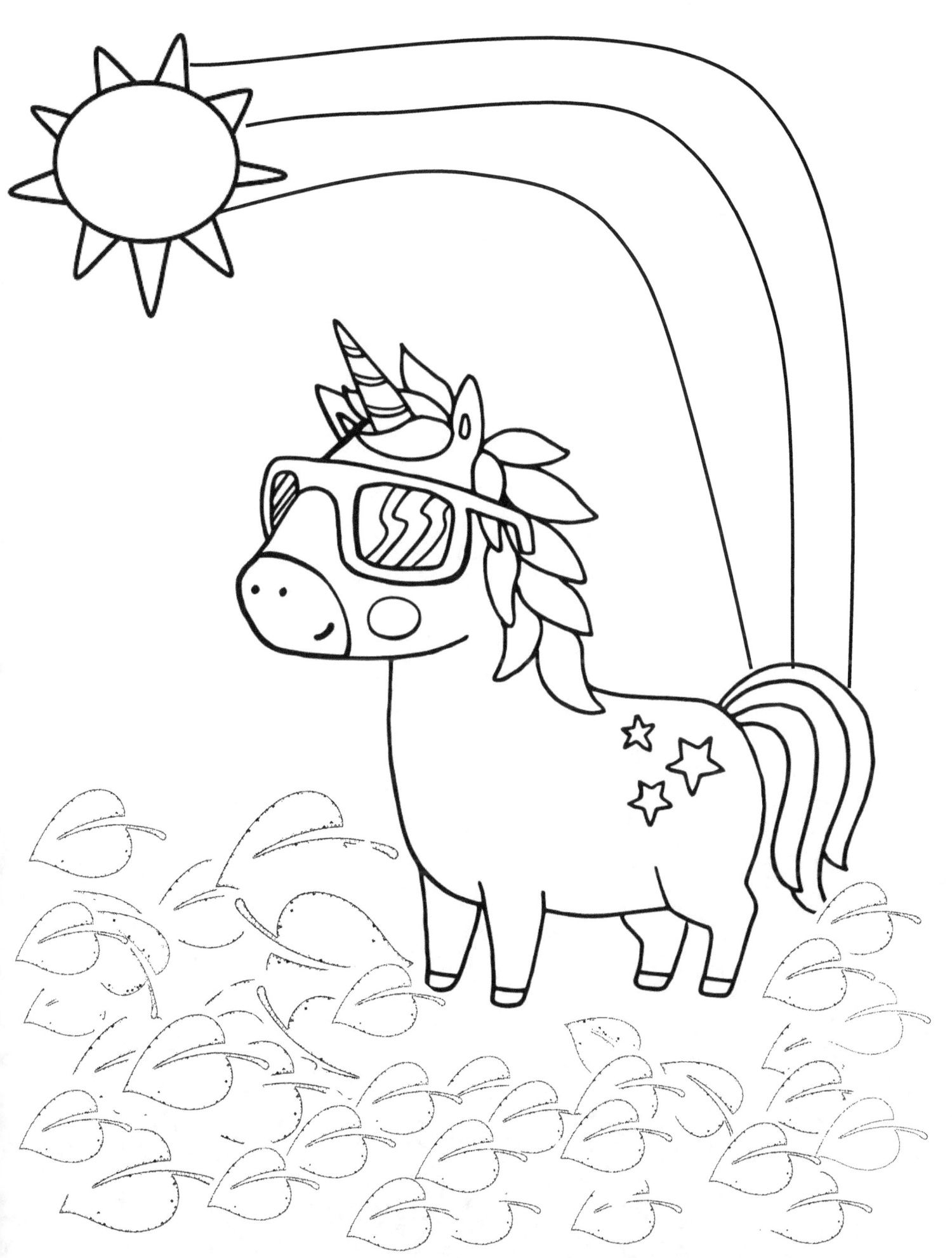

UNICORN

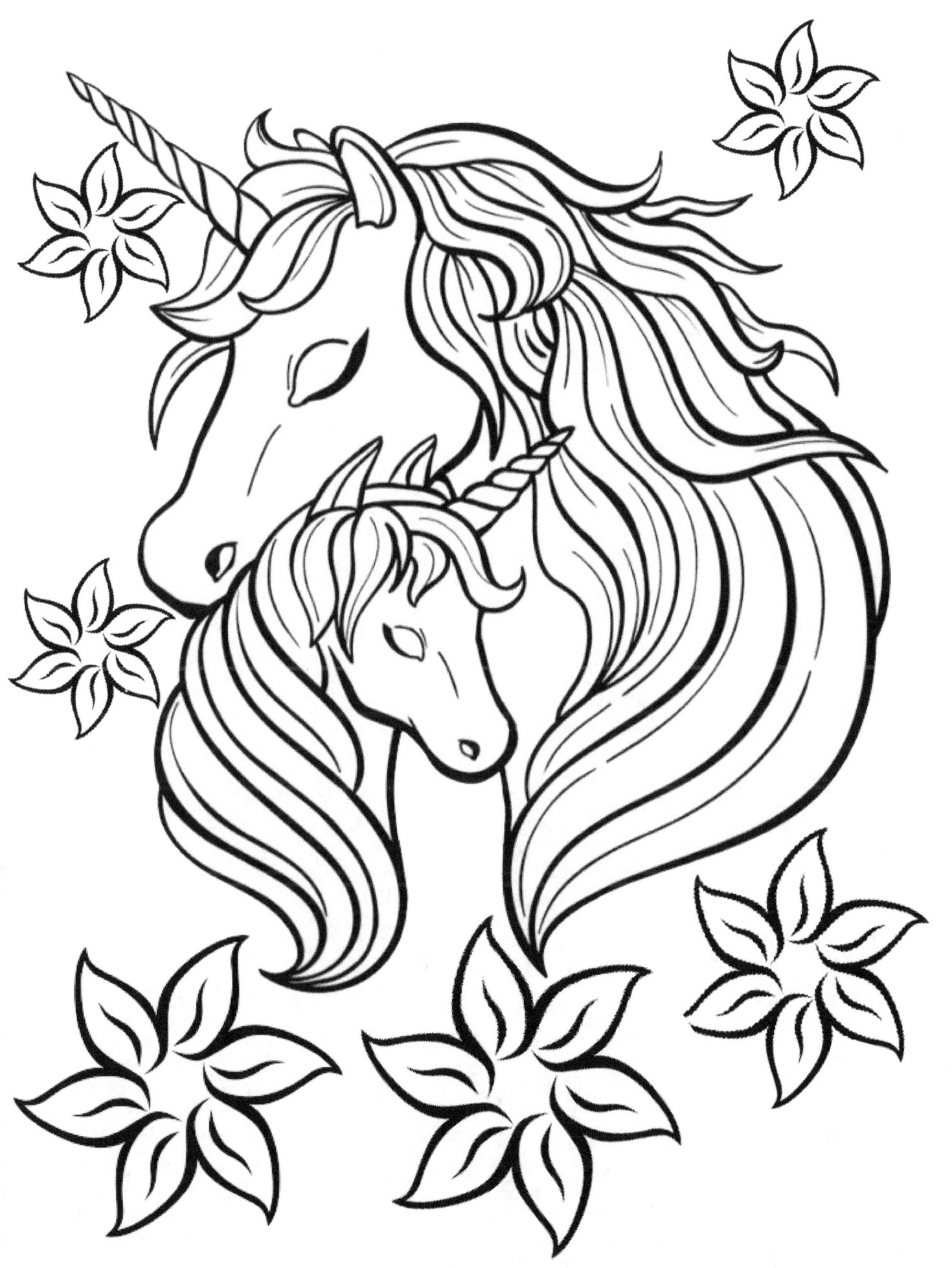

UNICORN

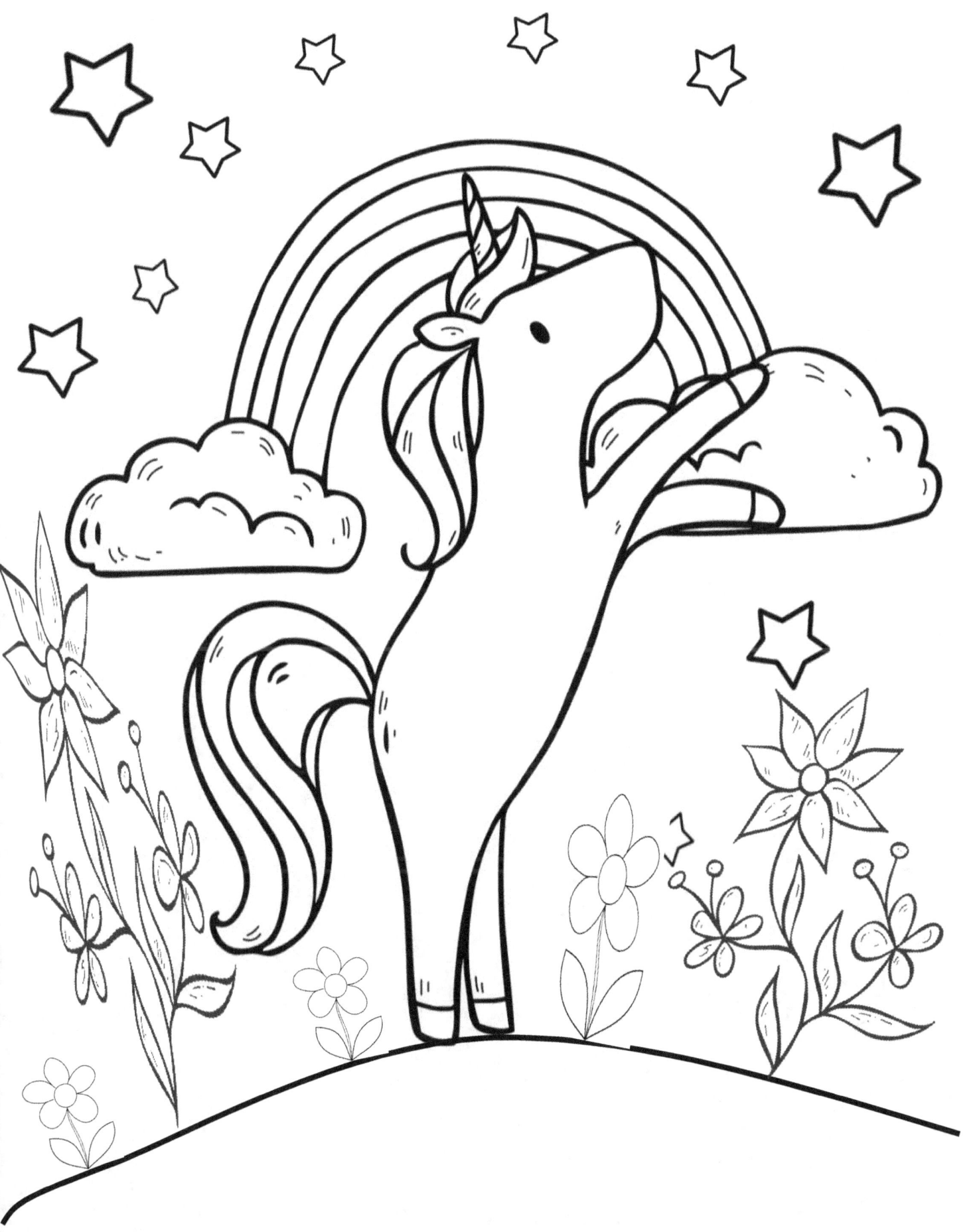

UNICORN

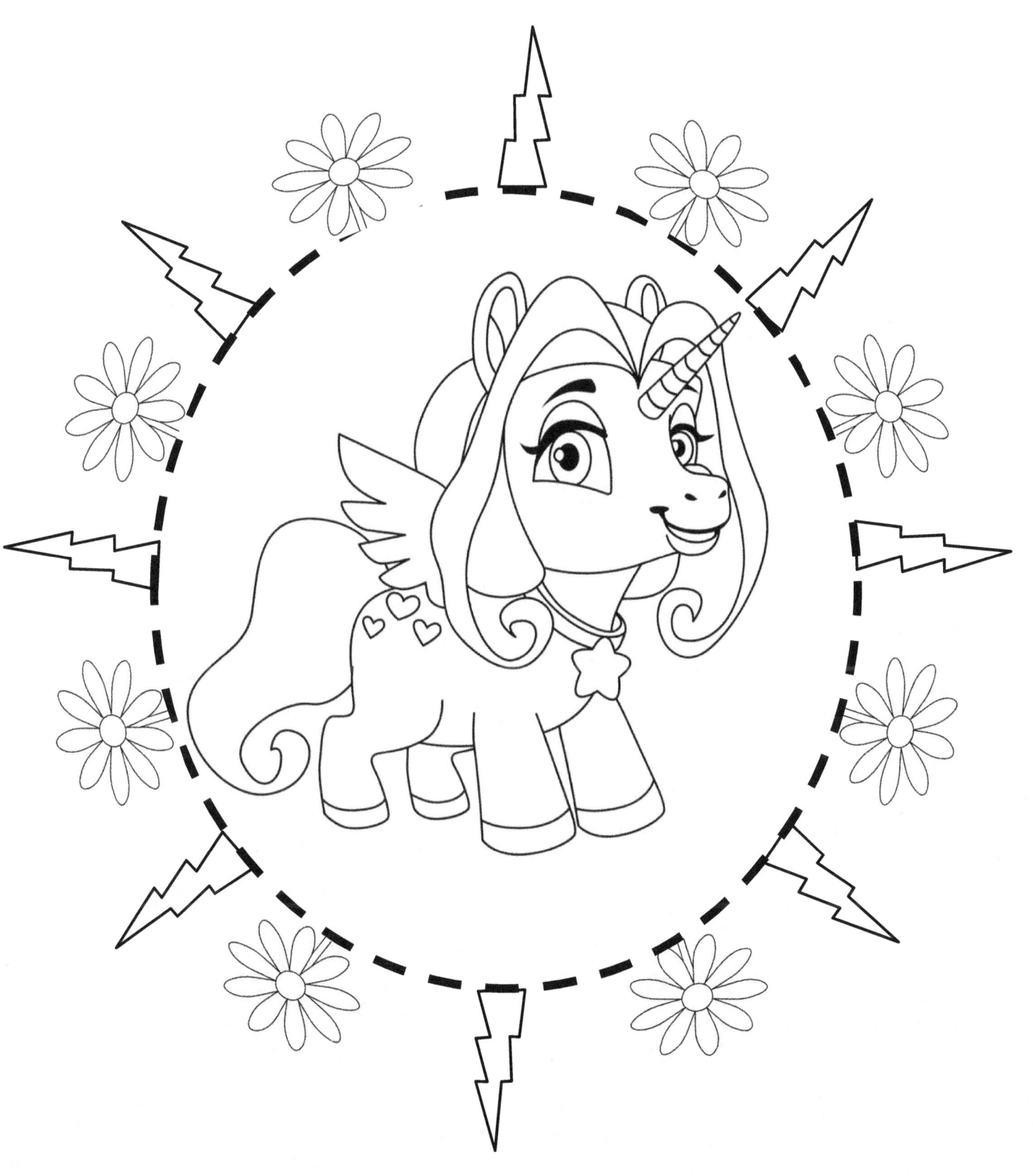

UNICORN

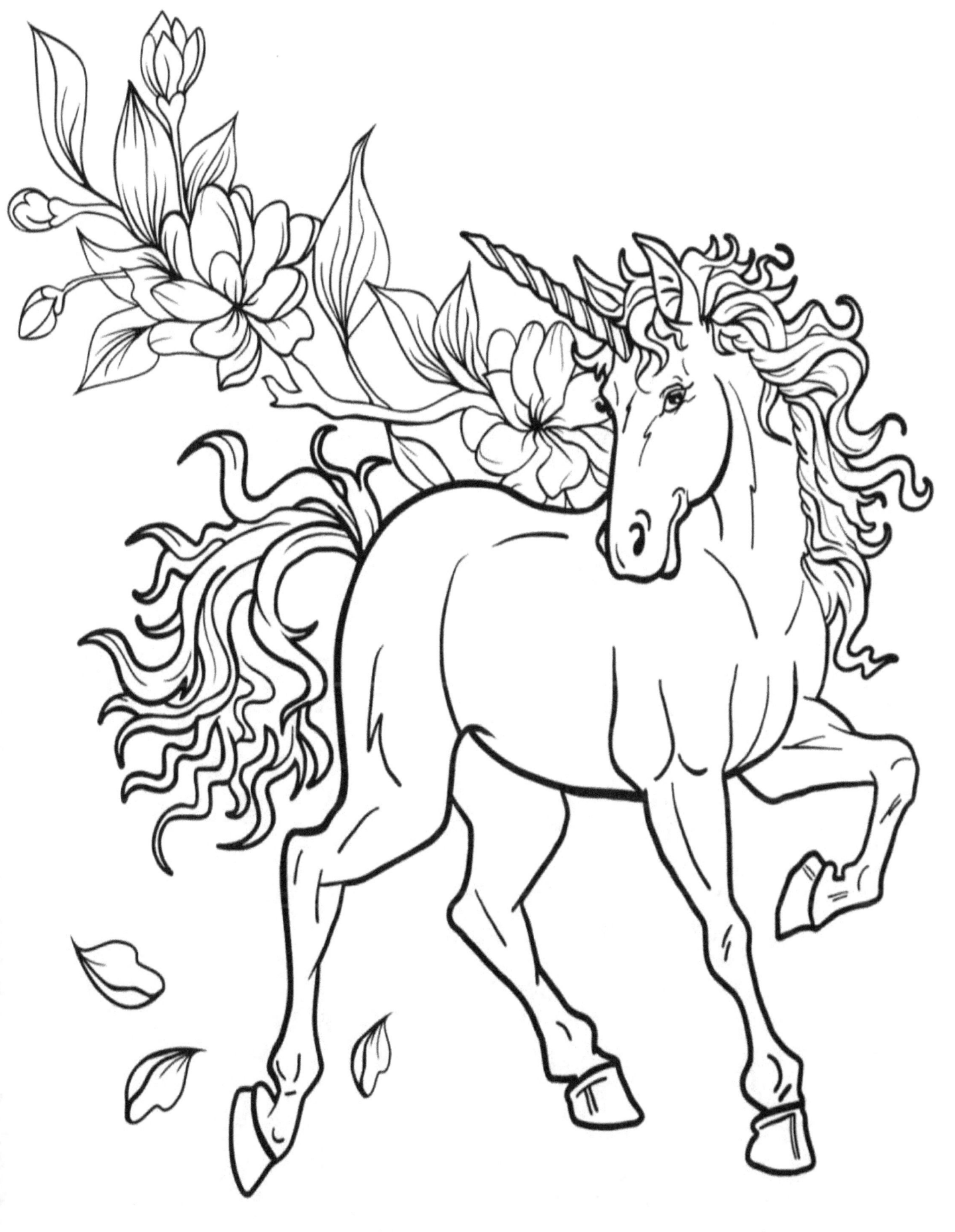

UNICORN

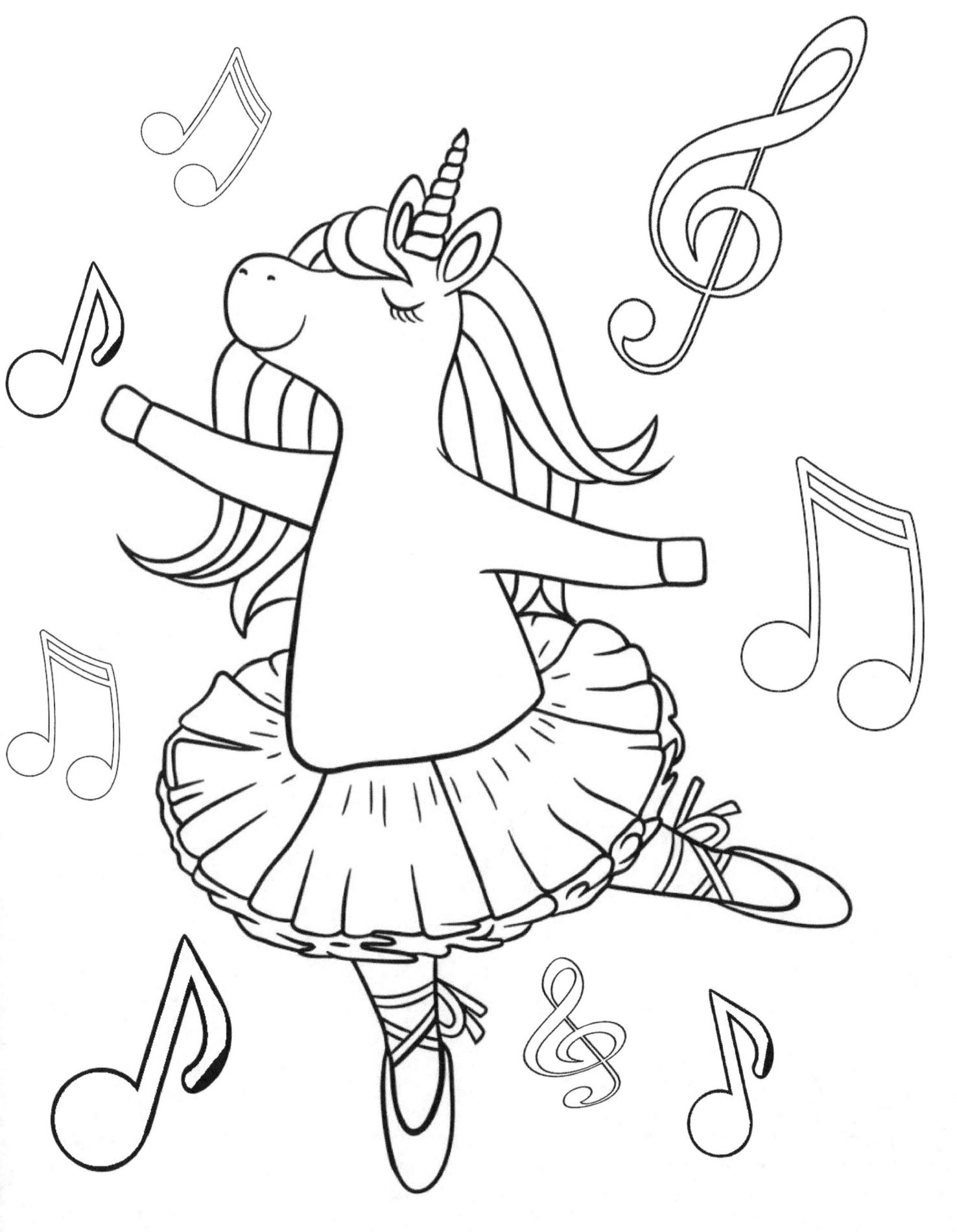

UNICORN

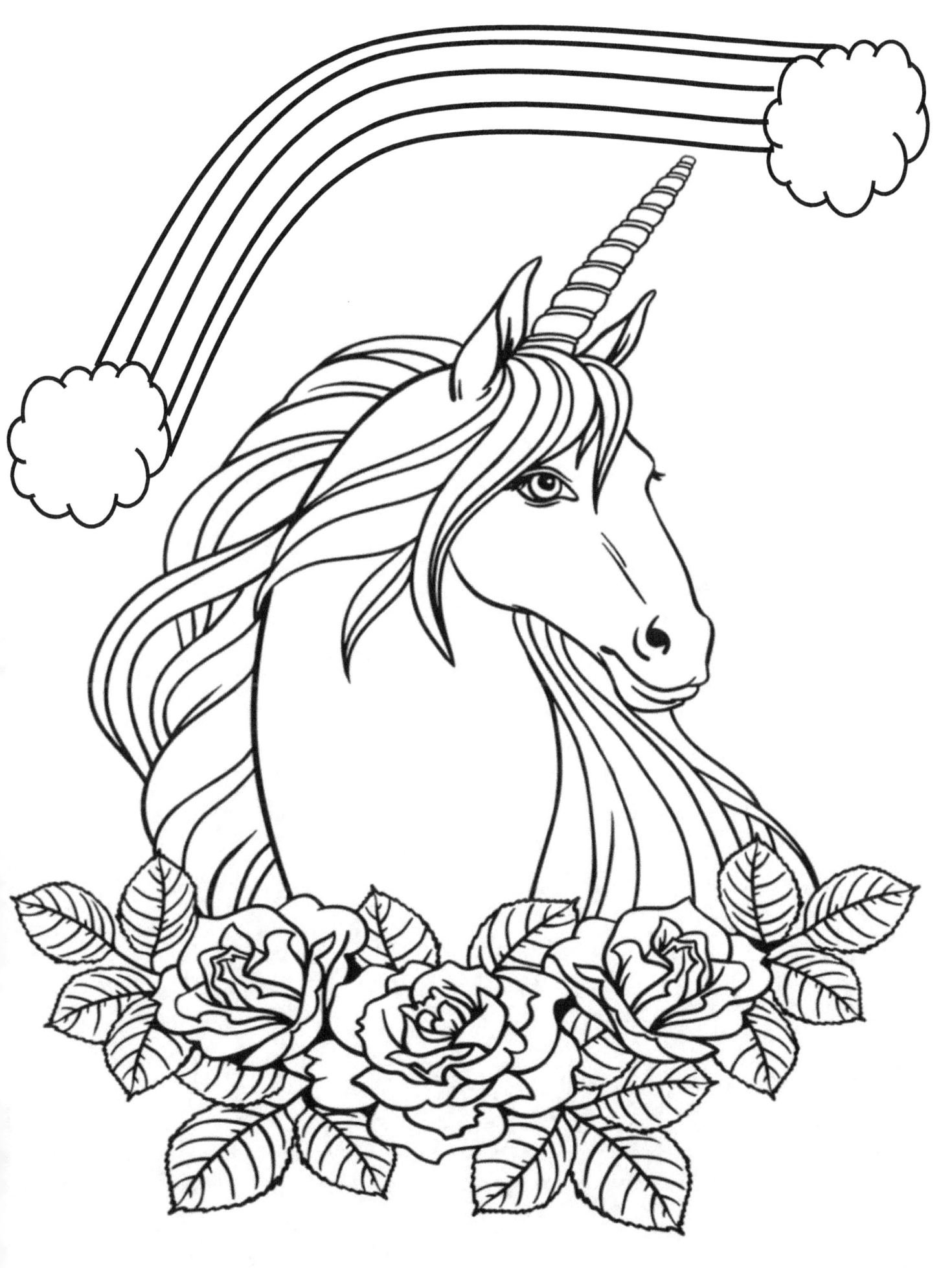

UNICORN

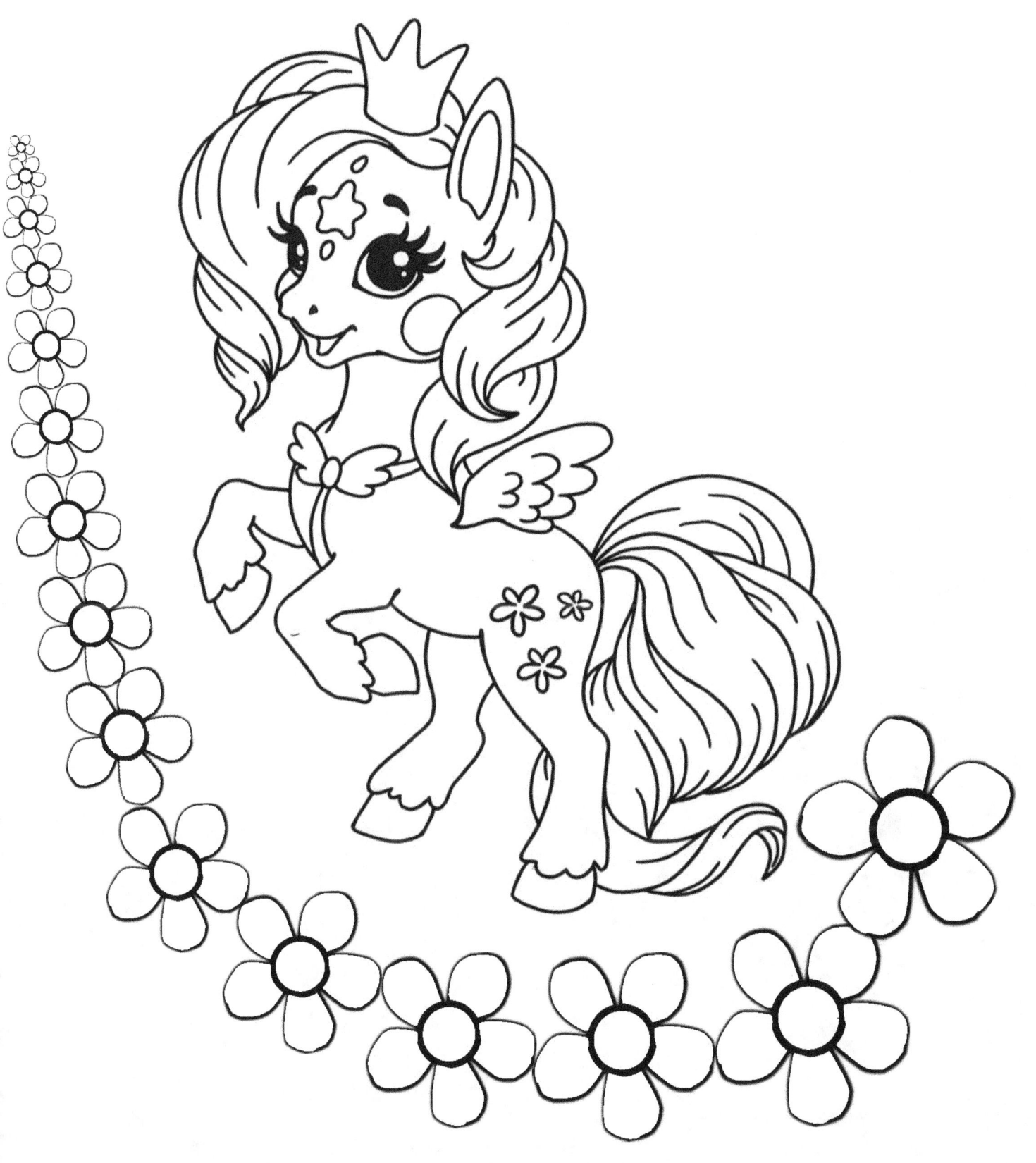

UNICORN

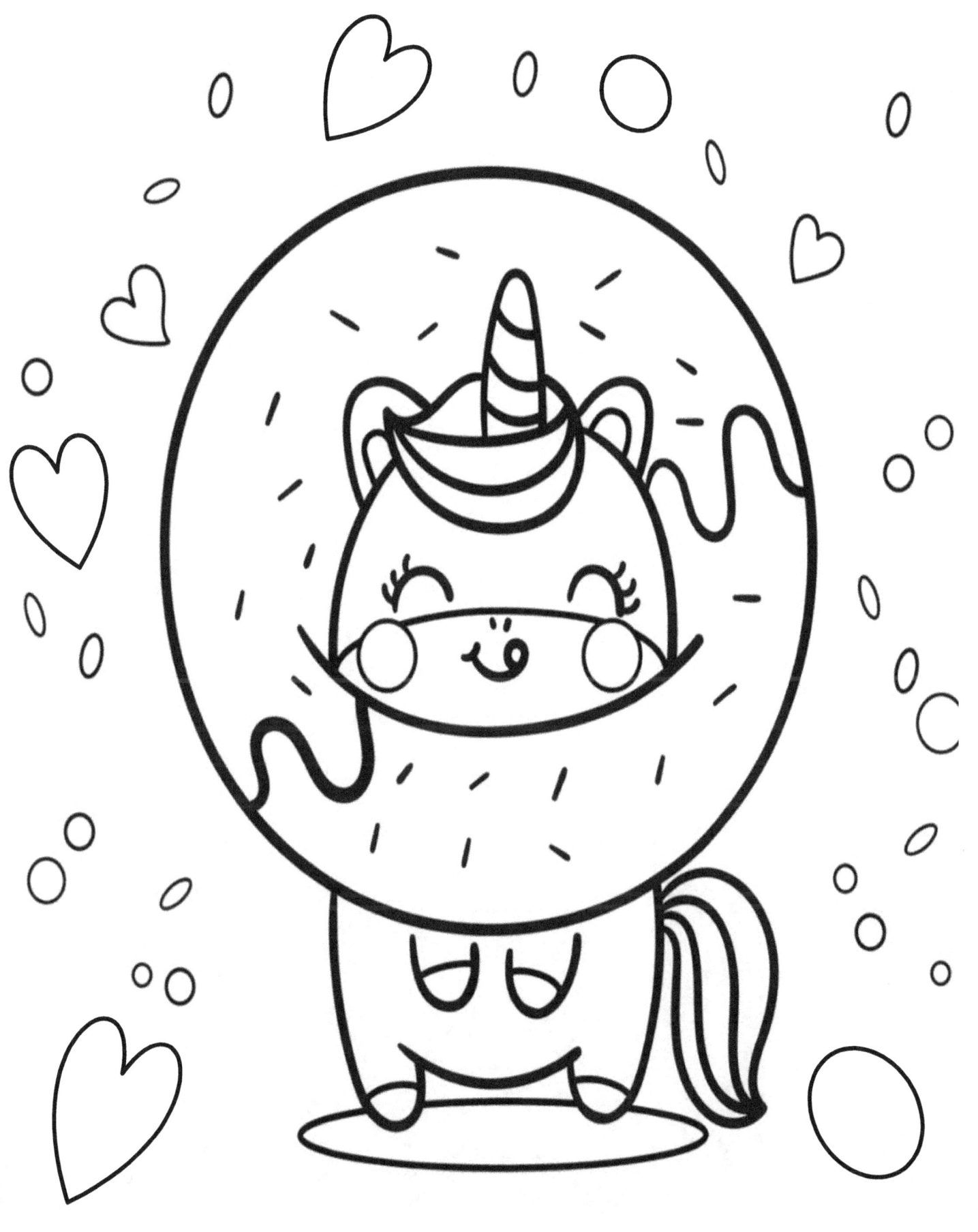

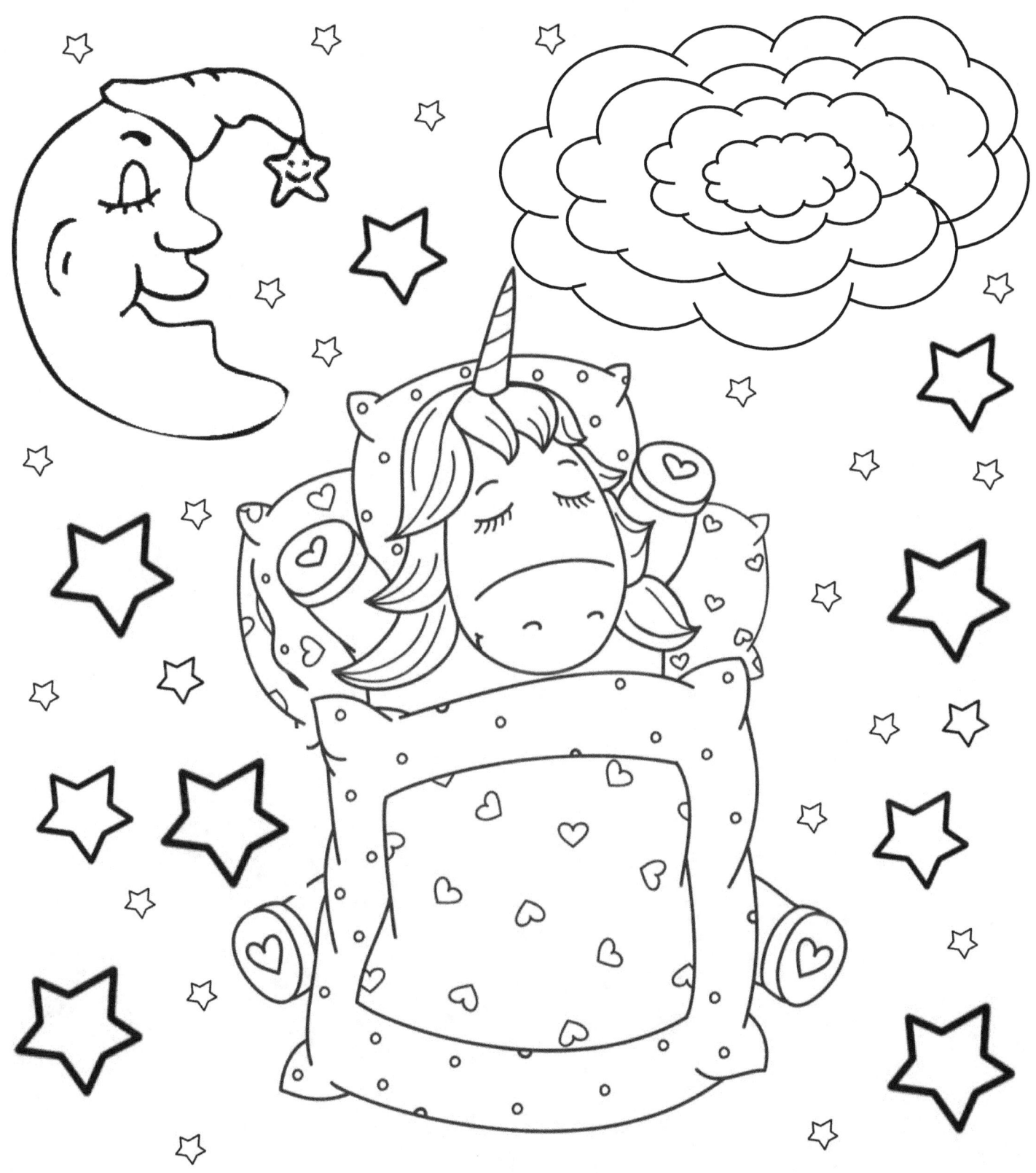

UNICORN

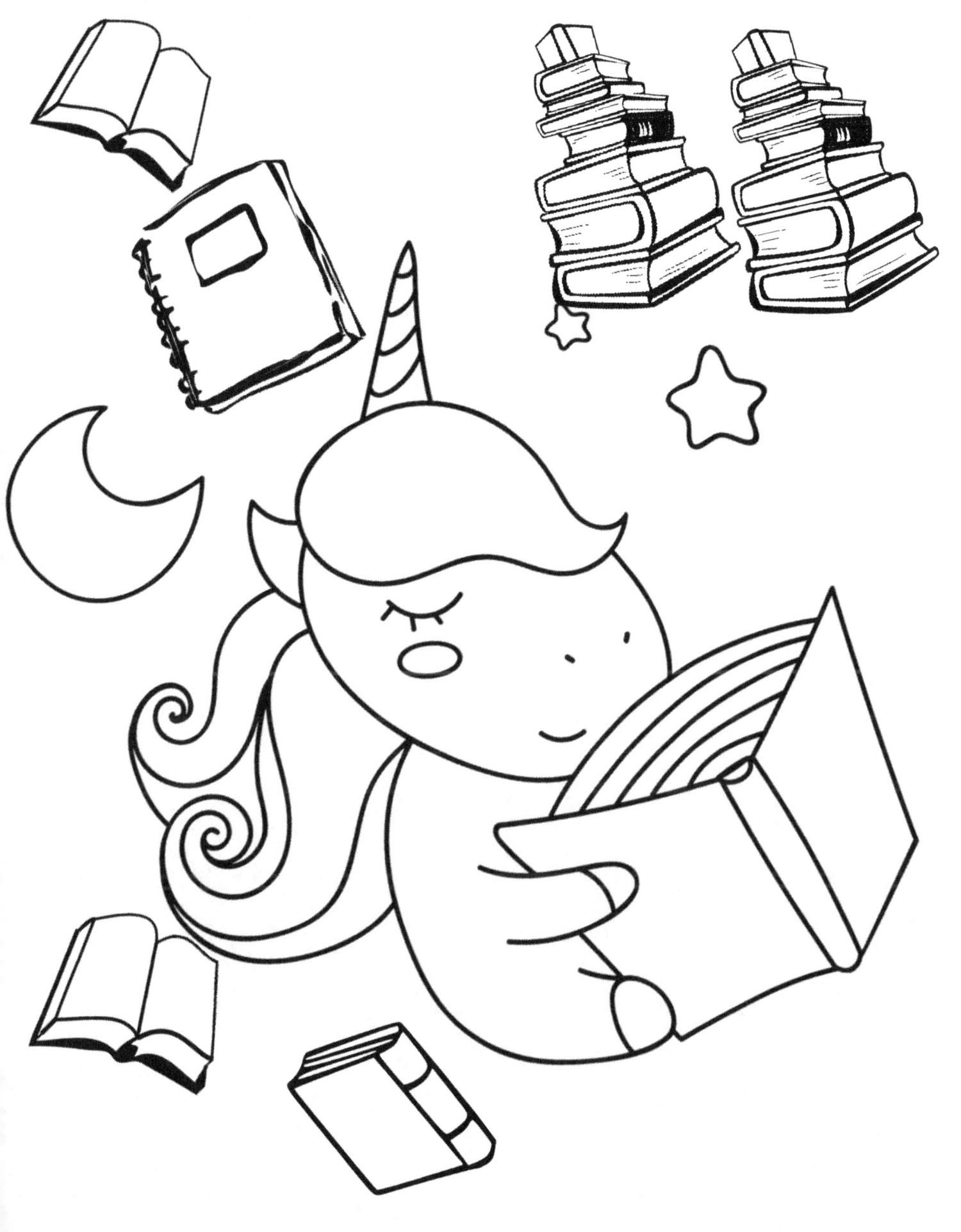

UNICORN

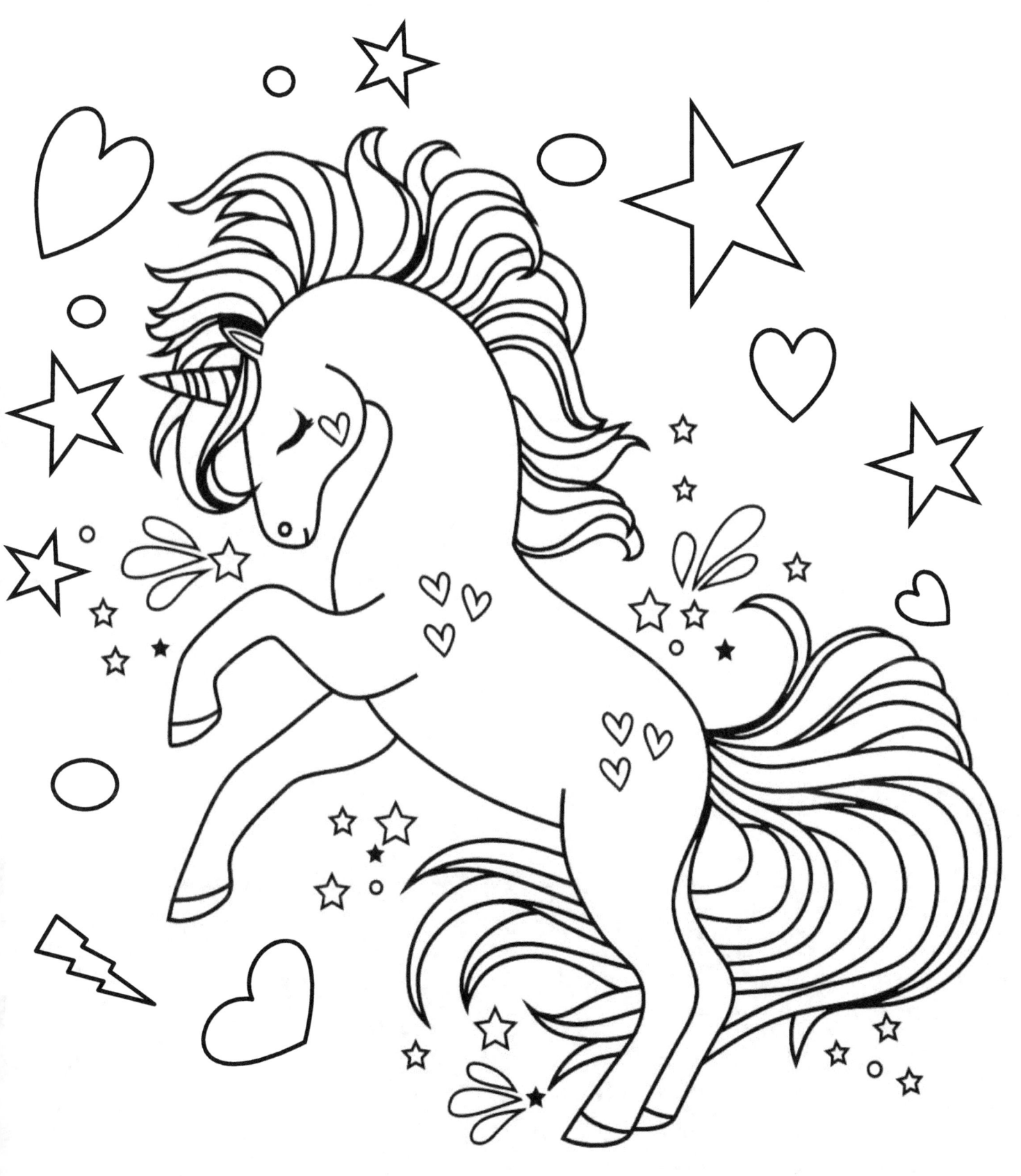

UNICORN

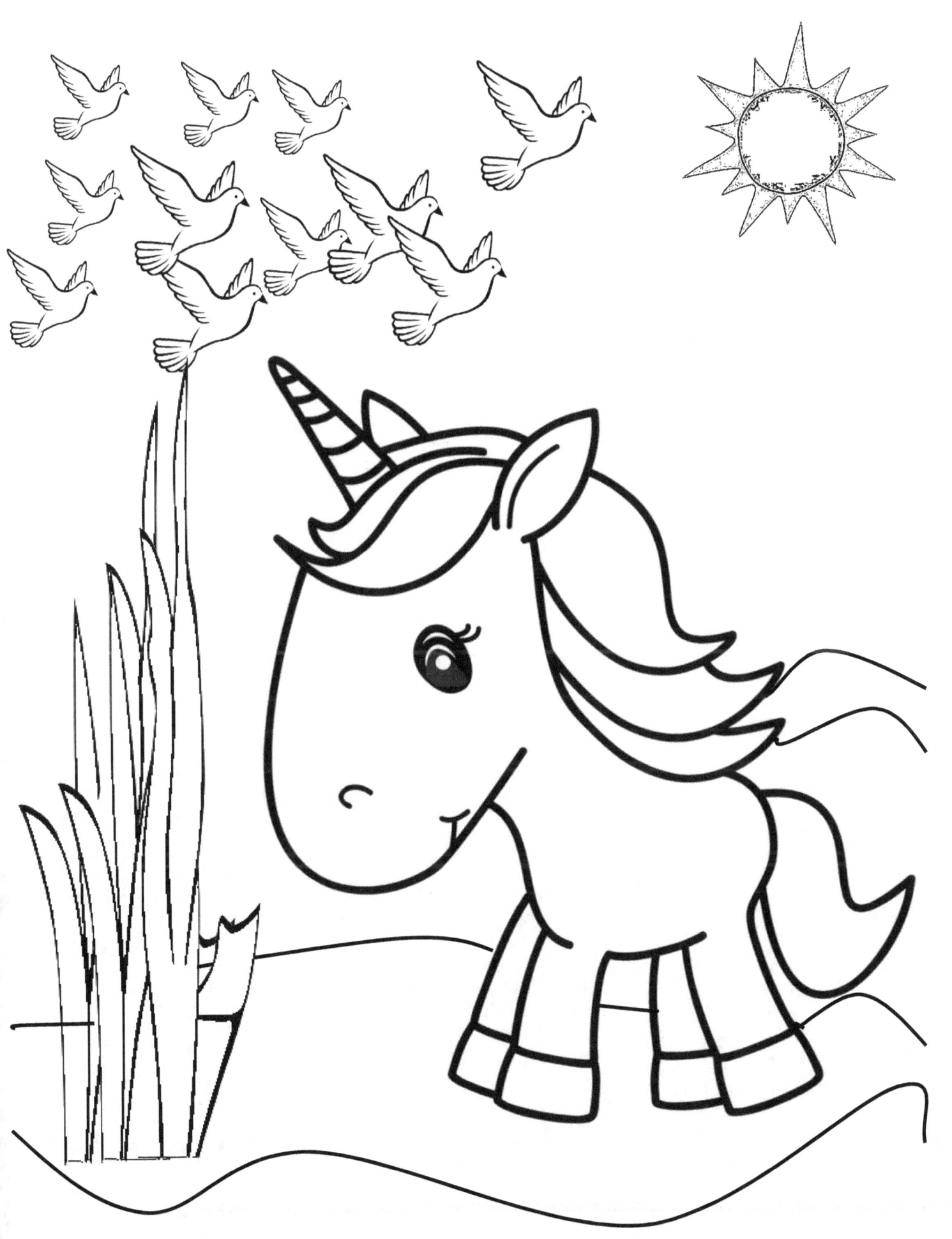

UNICORN

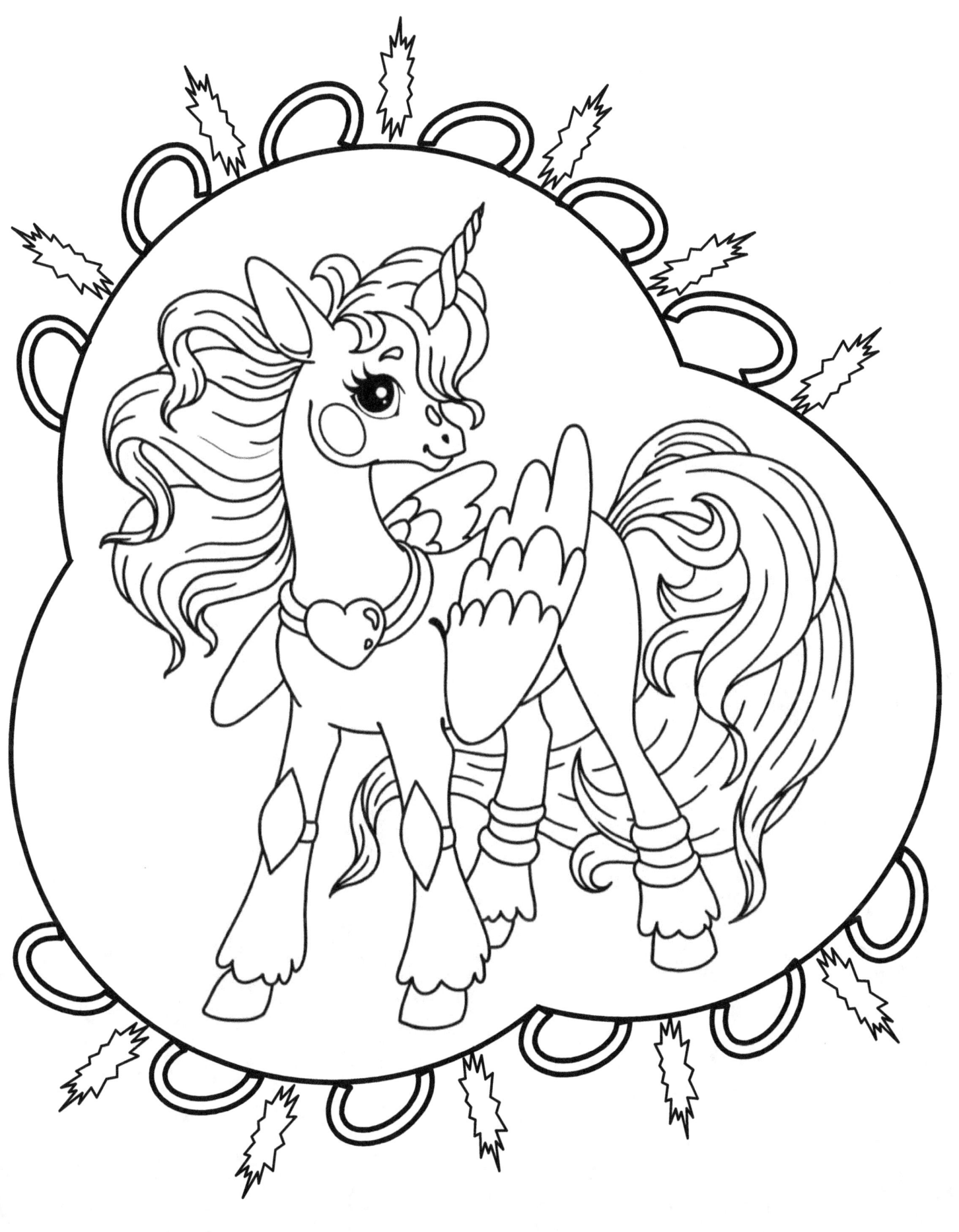

UNICORN

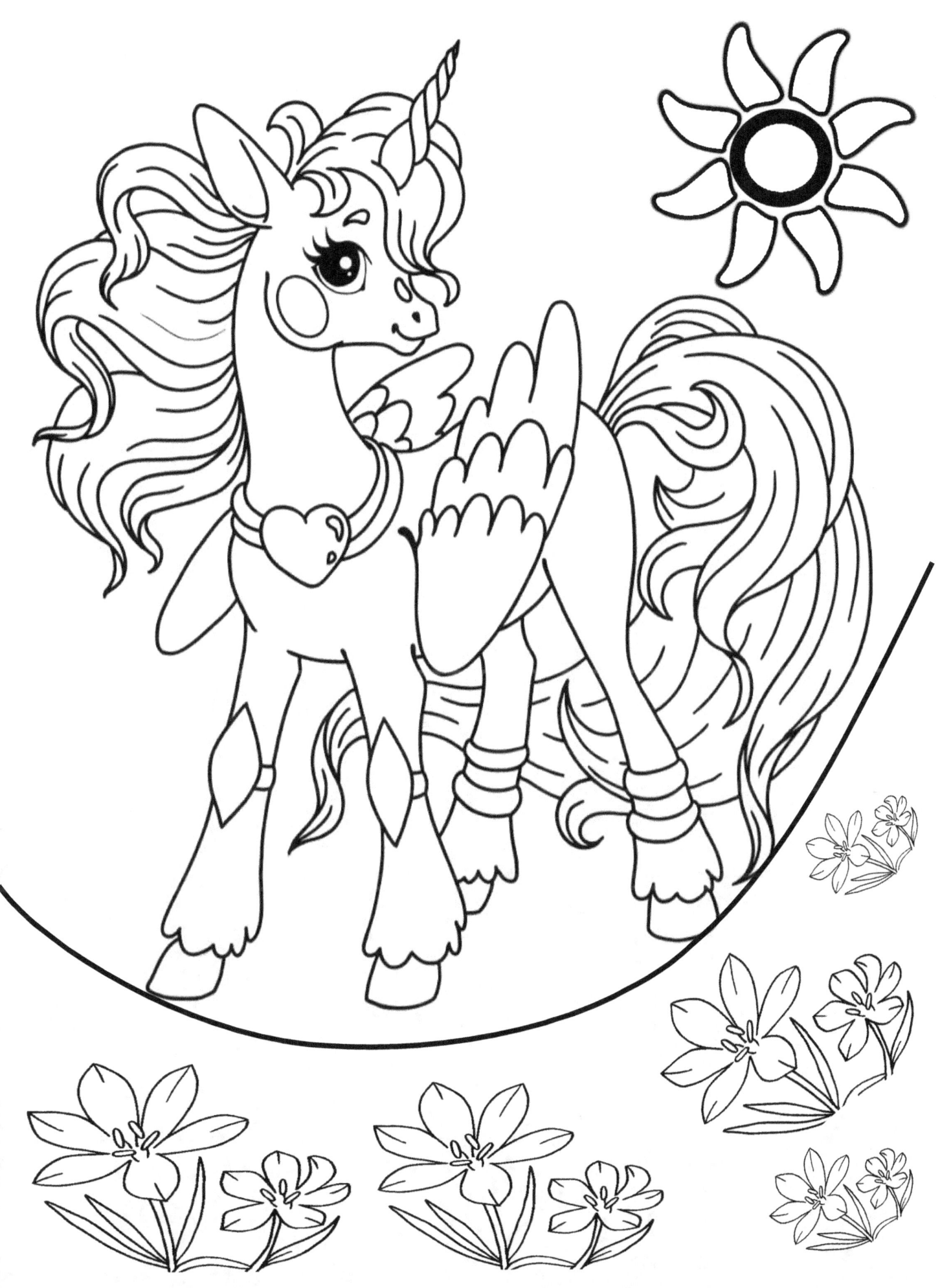

UNICORN

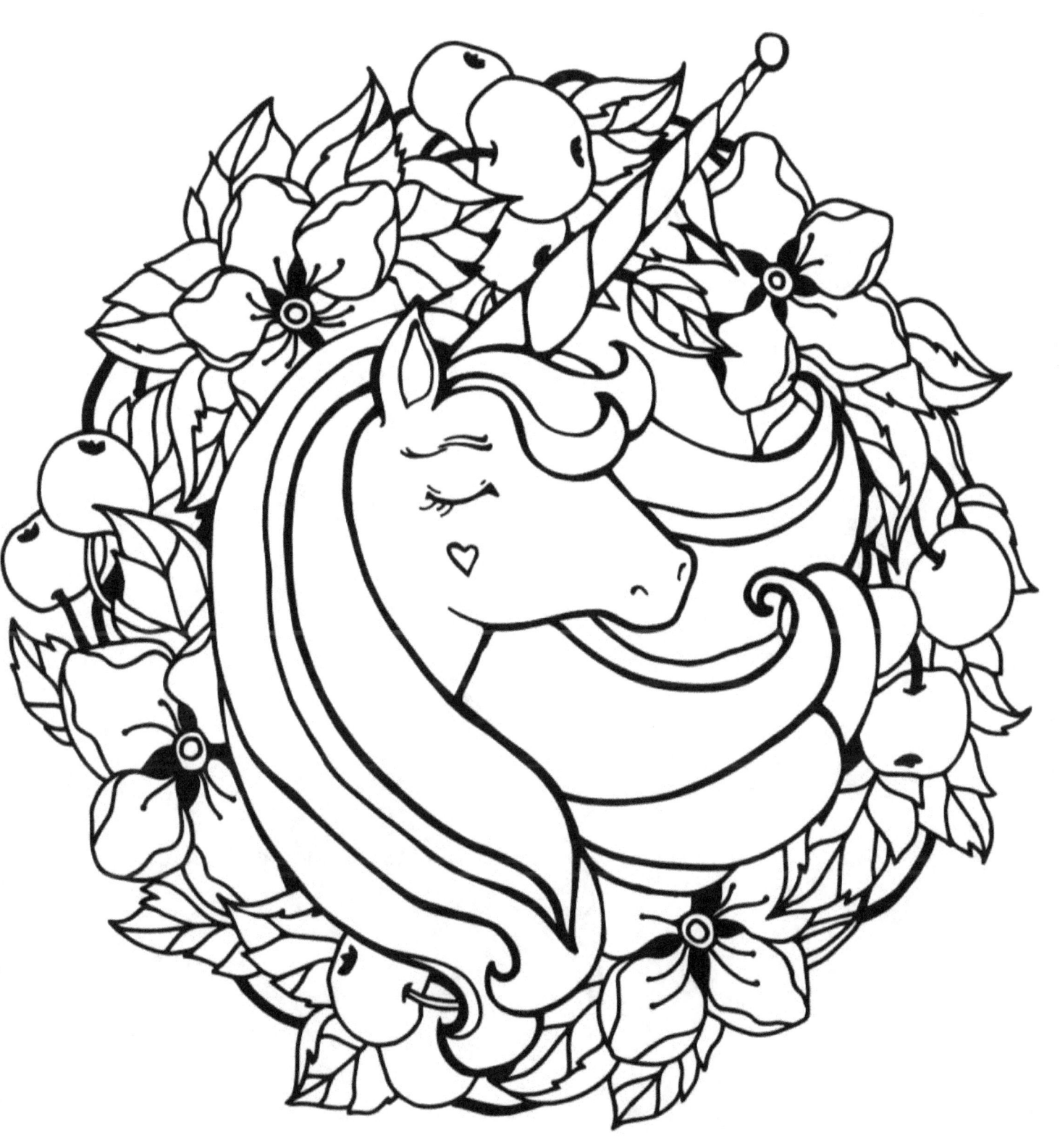

UNICORN

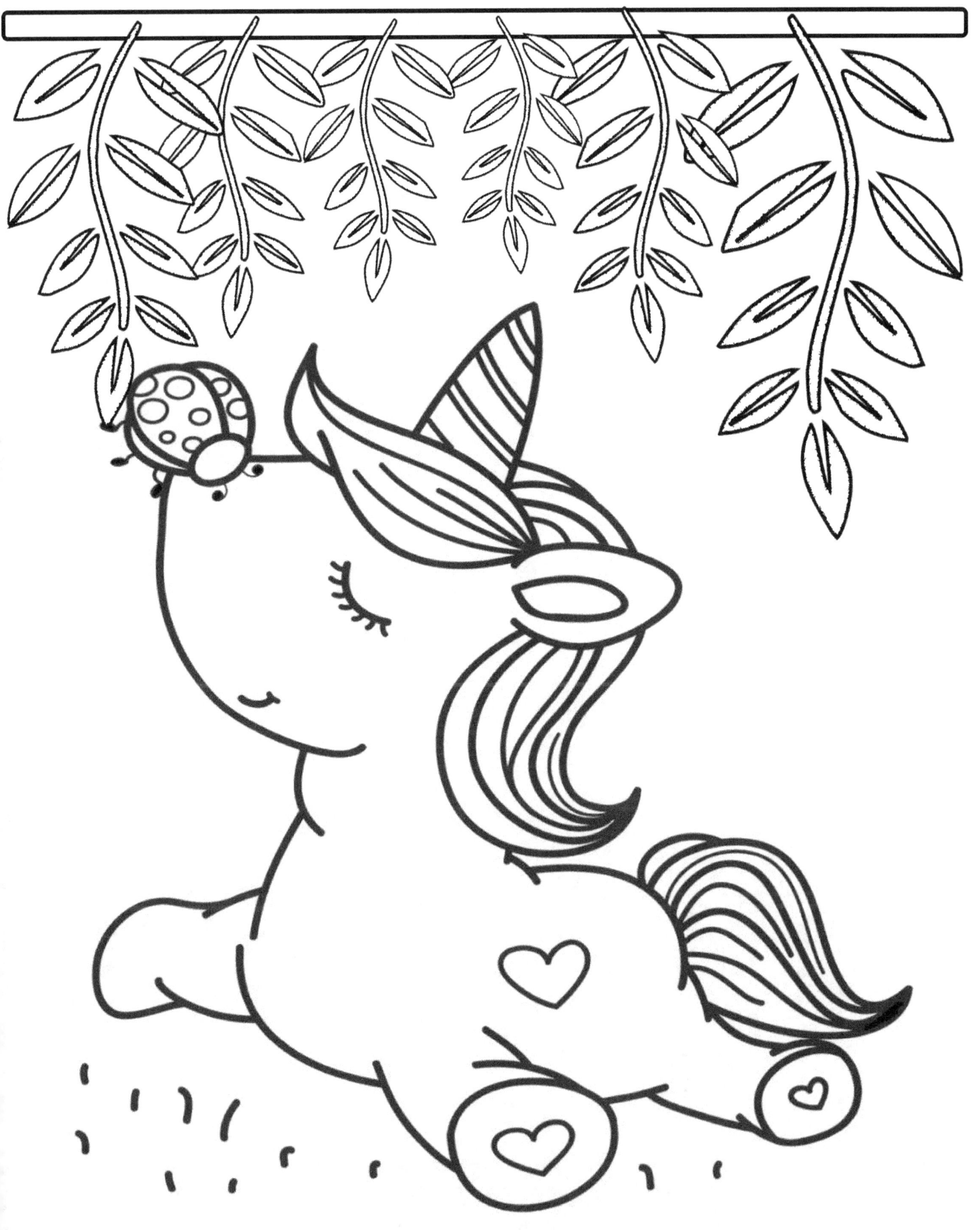

UNICORN

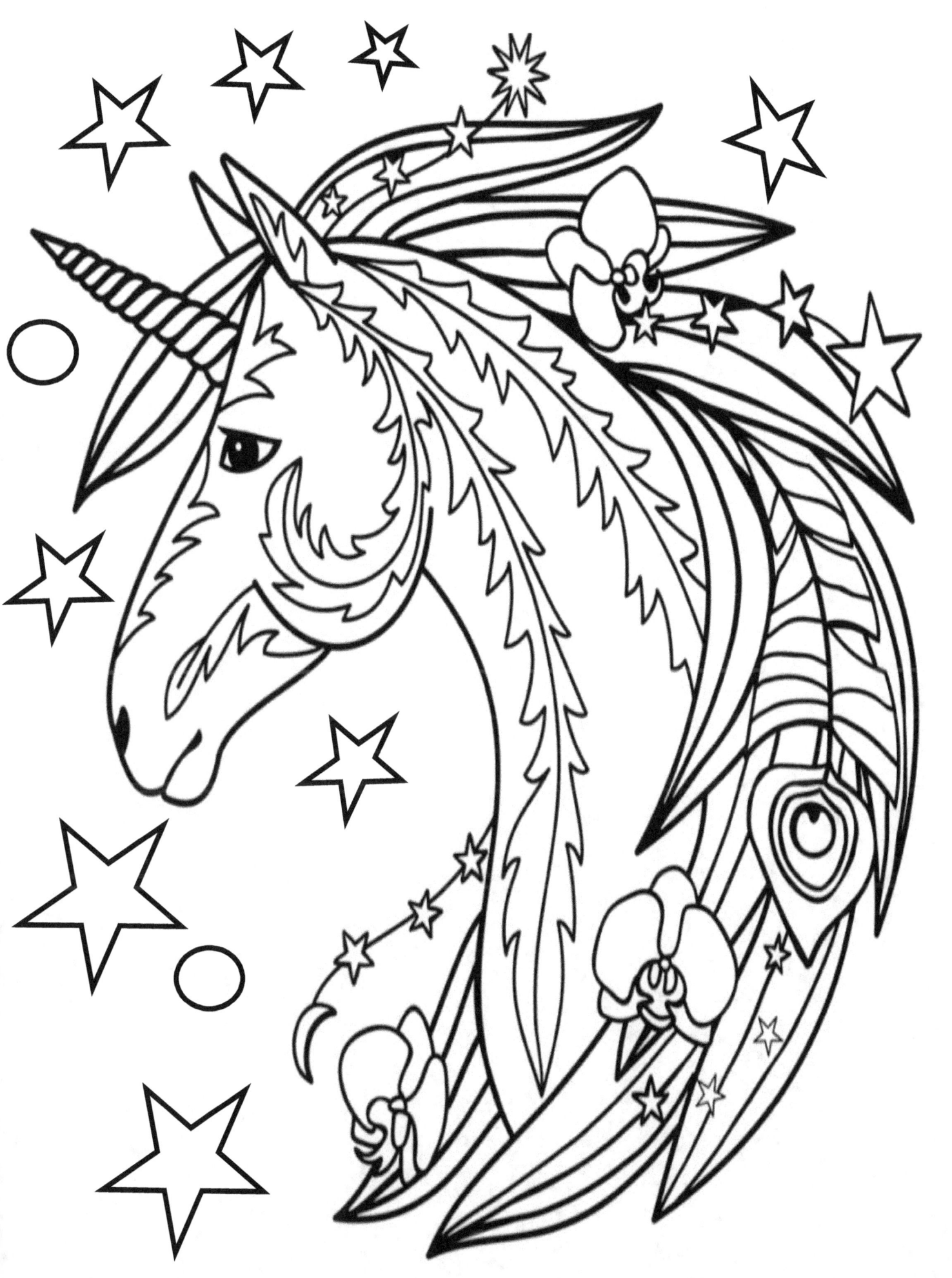

UNICORN

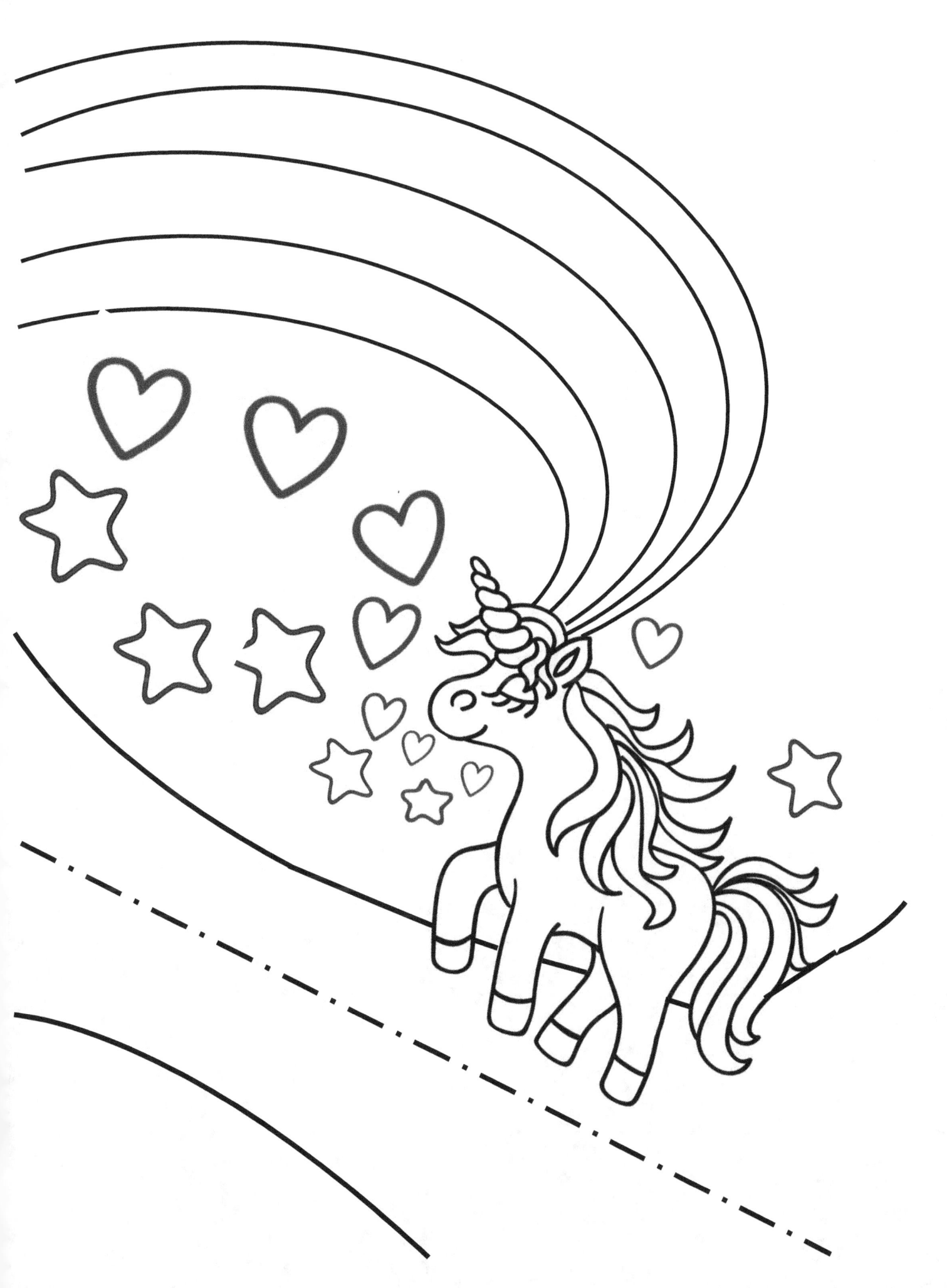

UNICORN

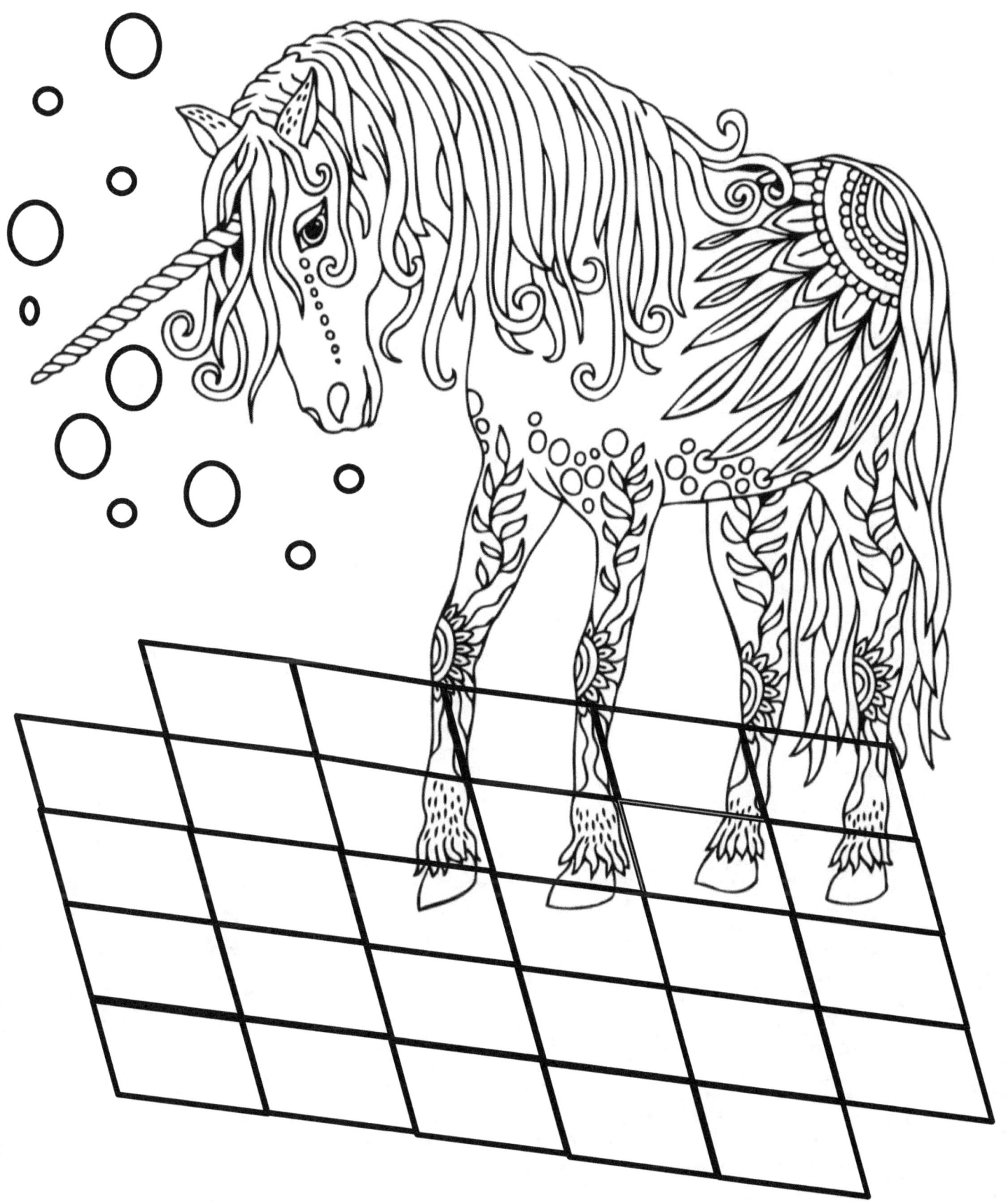

UNICORN

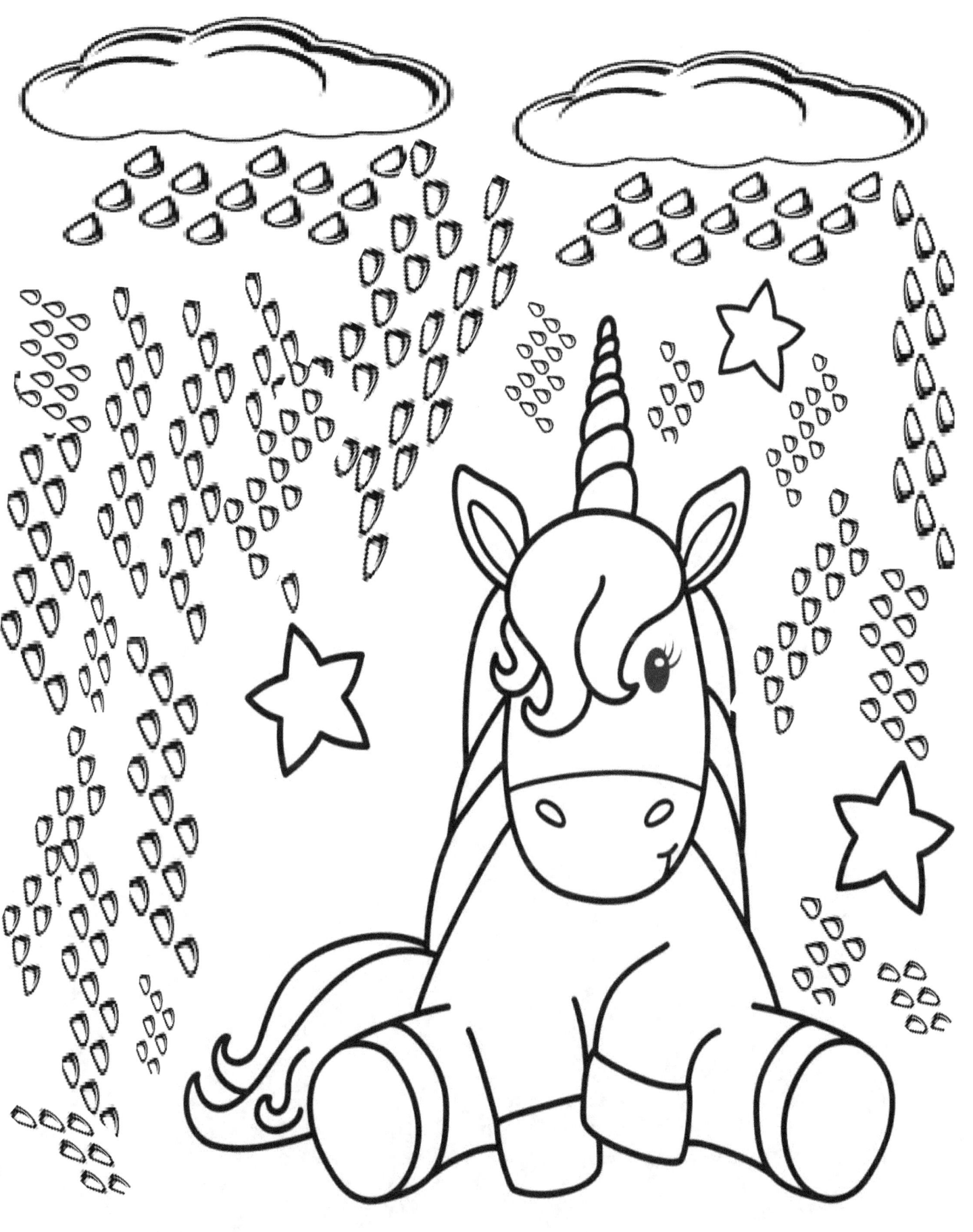

UNICORN

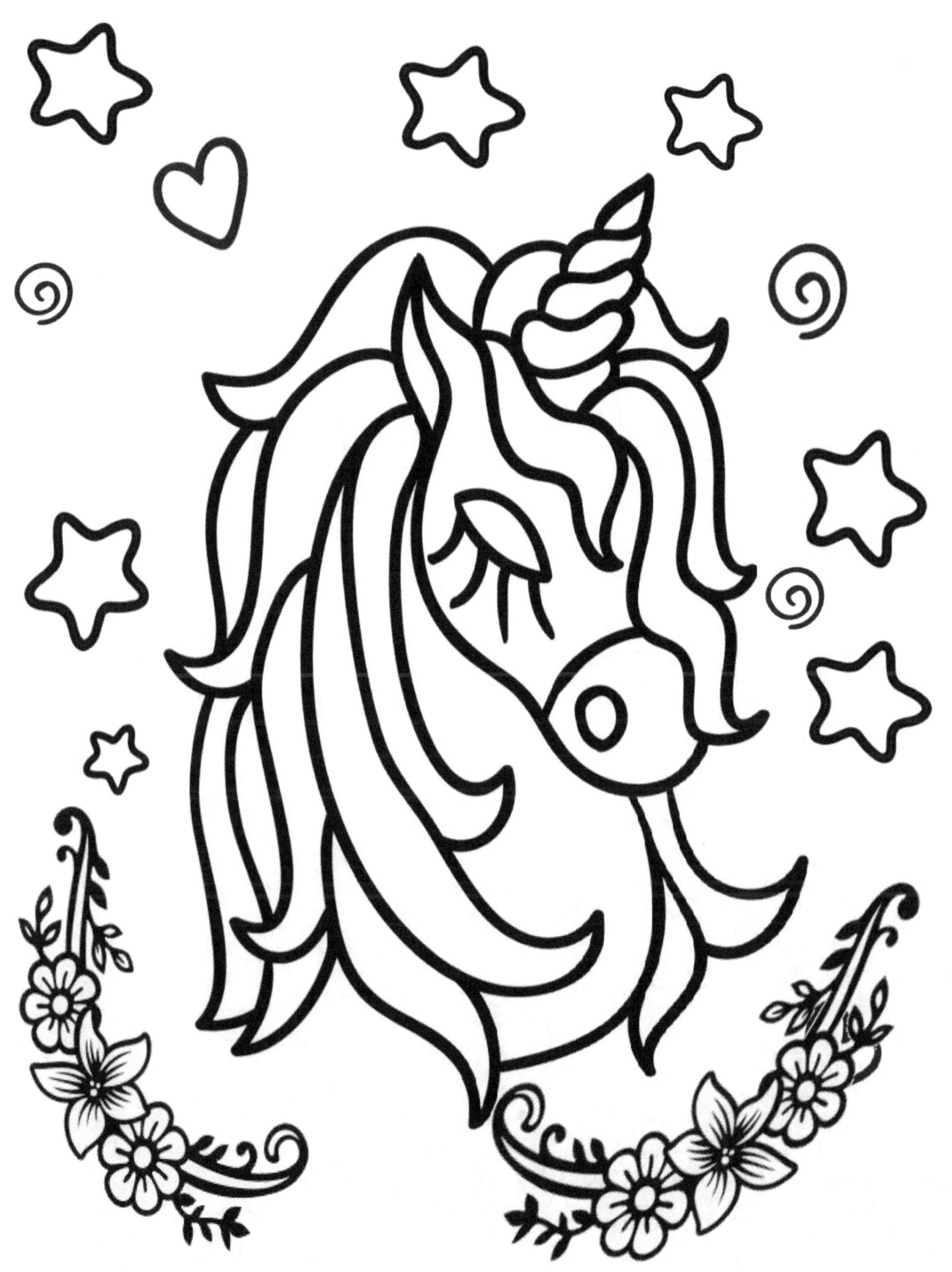

UNICORN

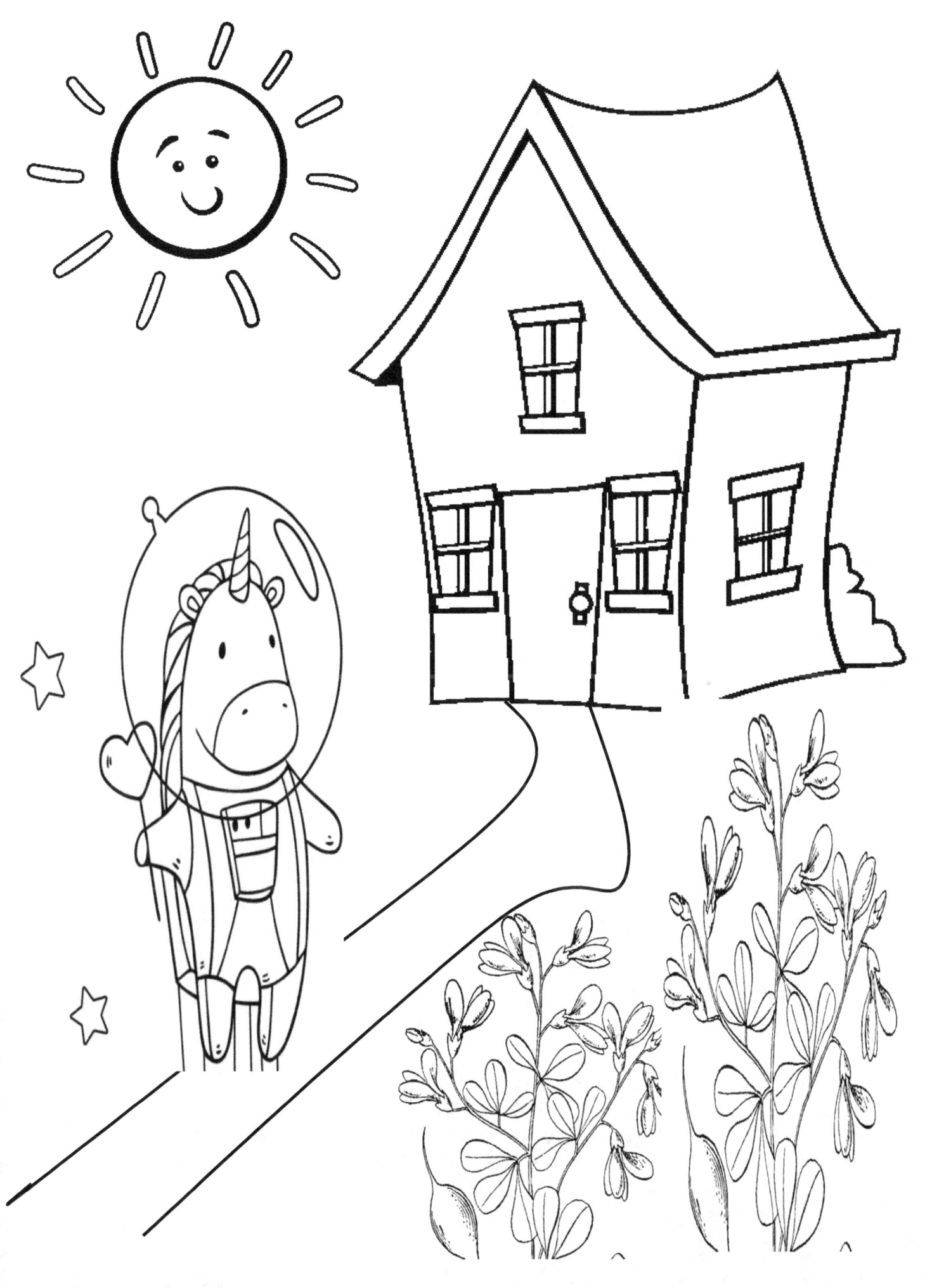

UNICORN

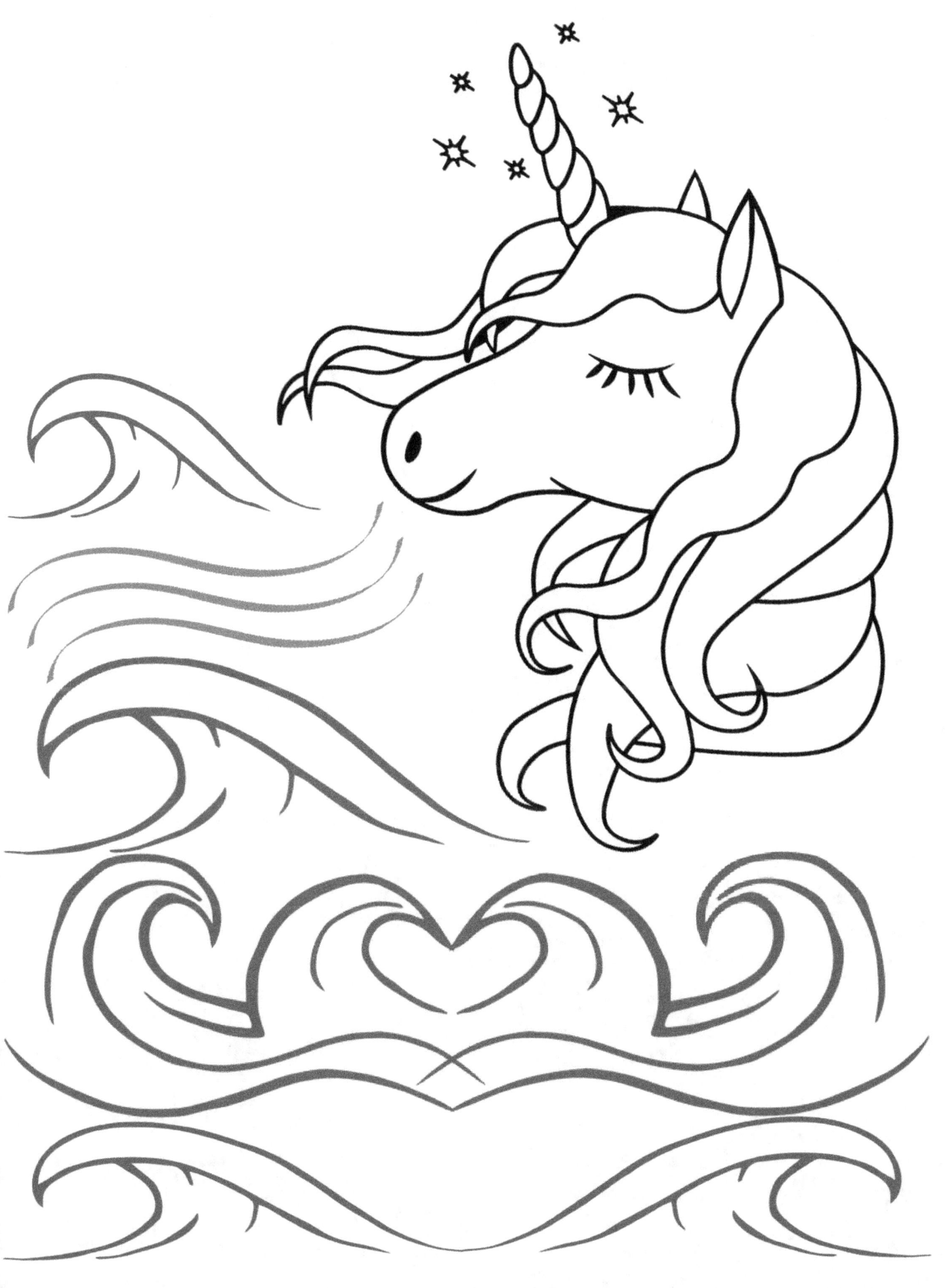

UNICORN

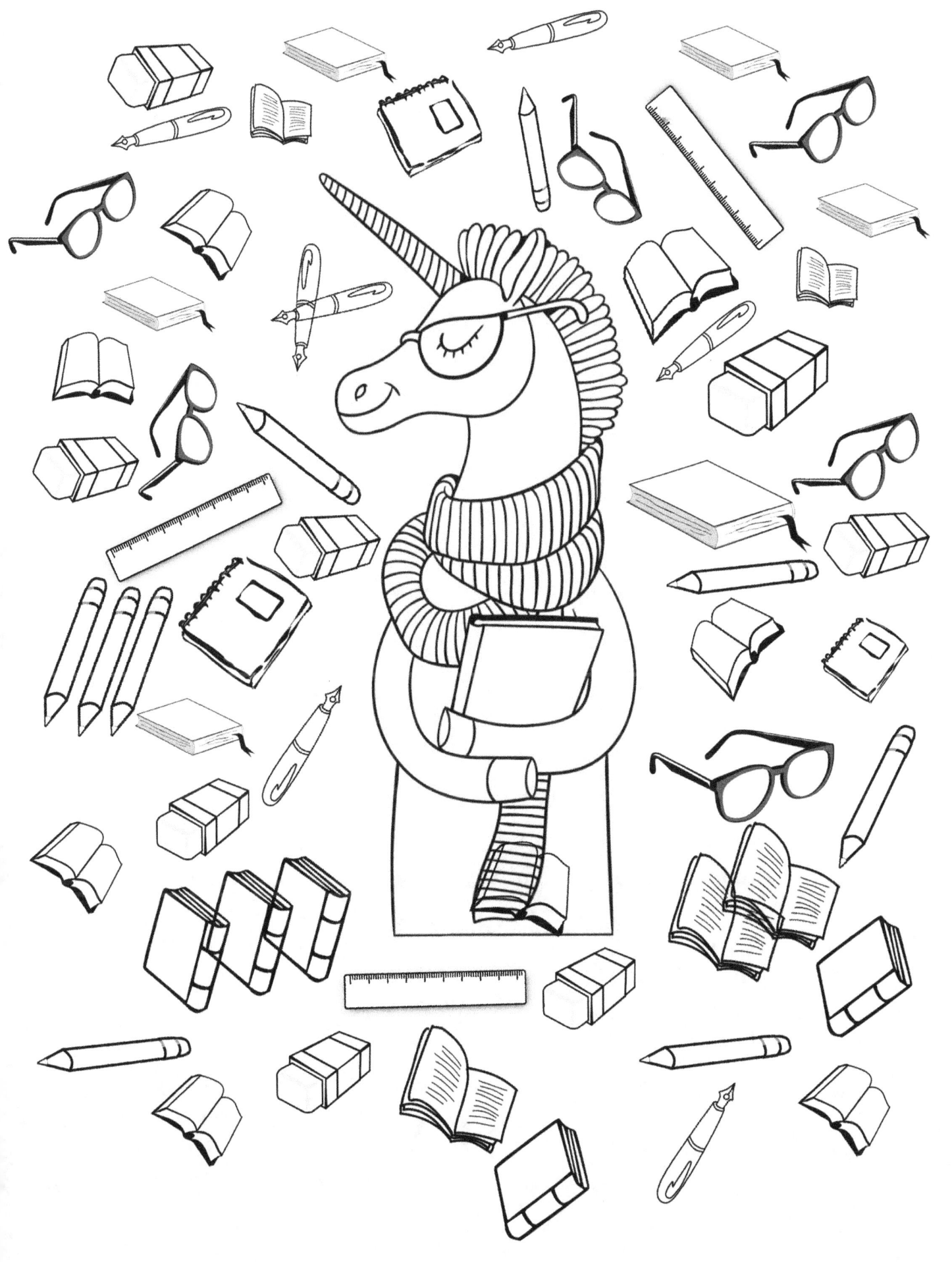

UNICORN

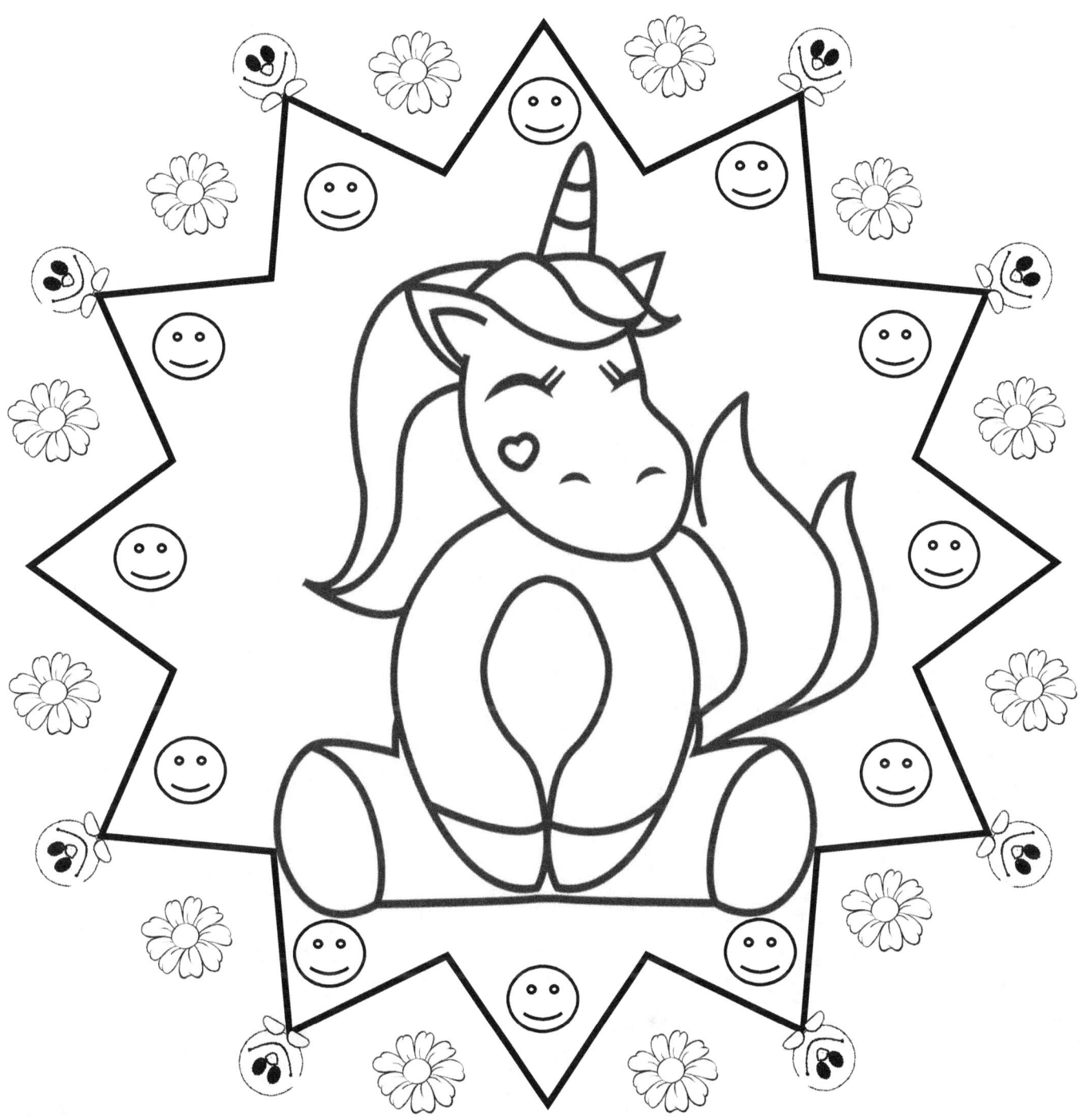

UNICORN

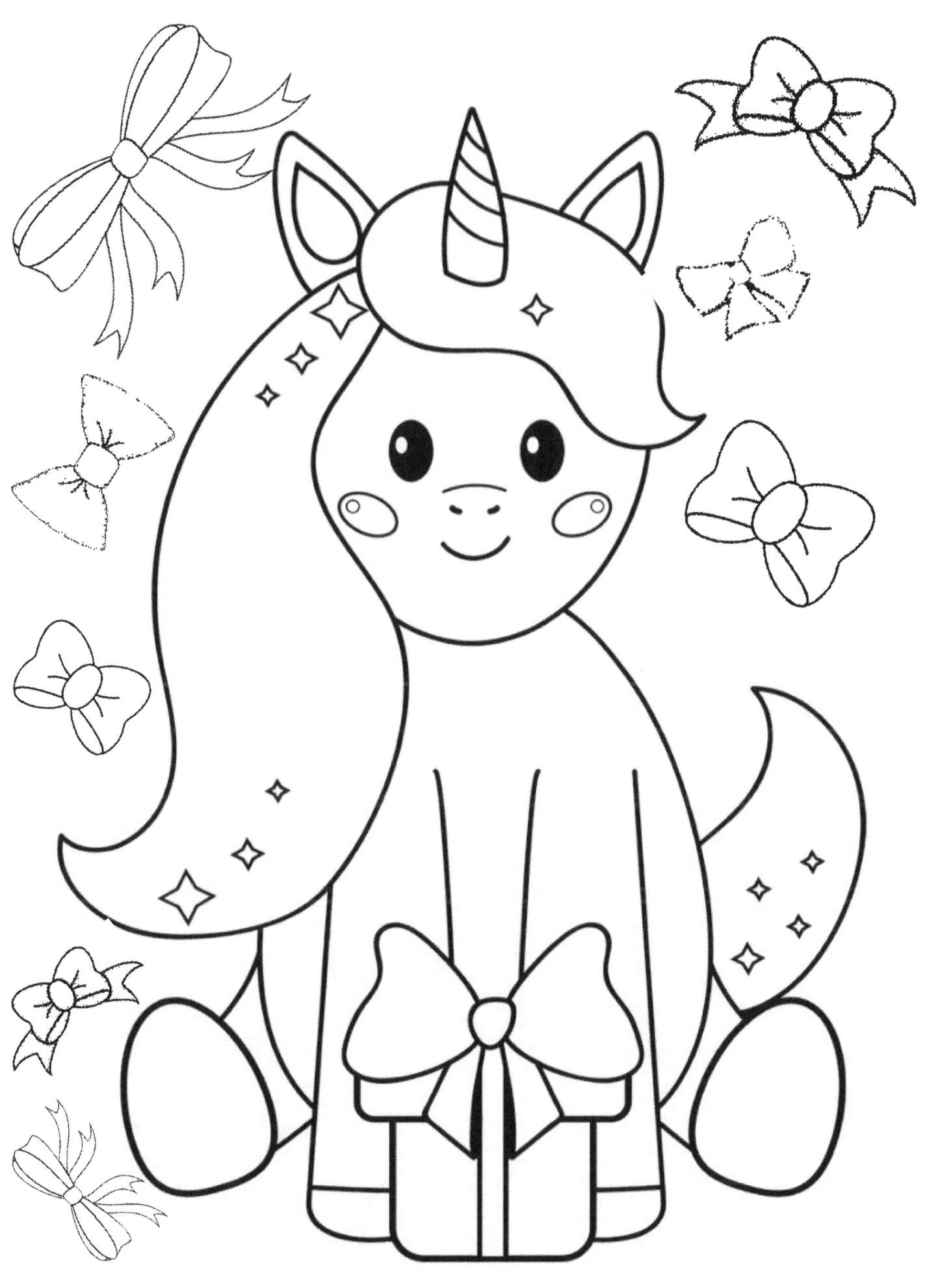

UNICORN

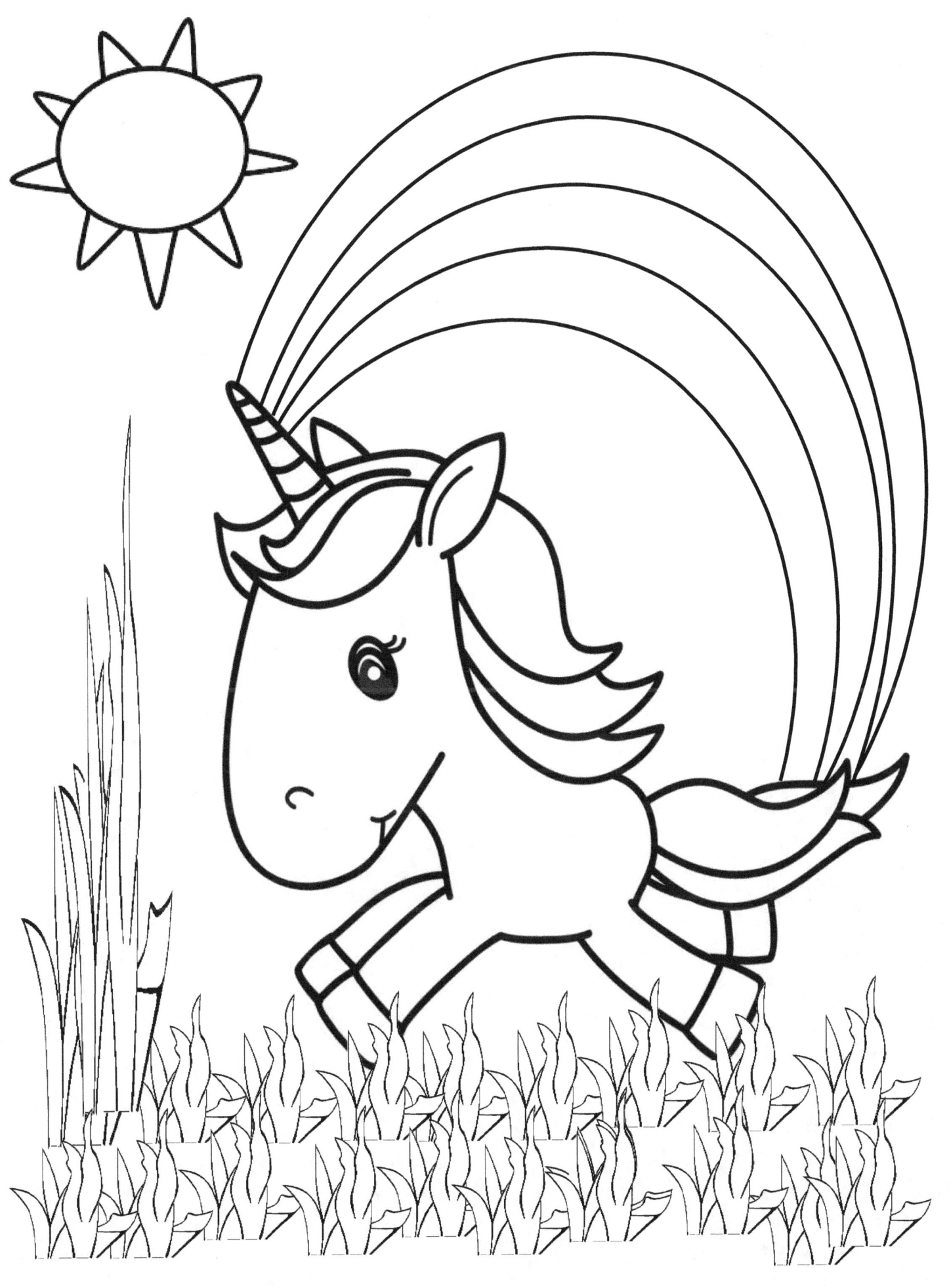

UNICORN

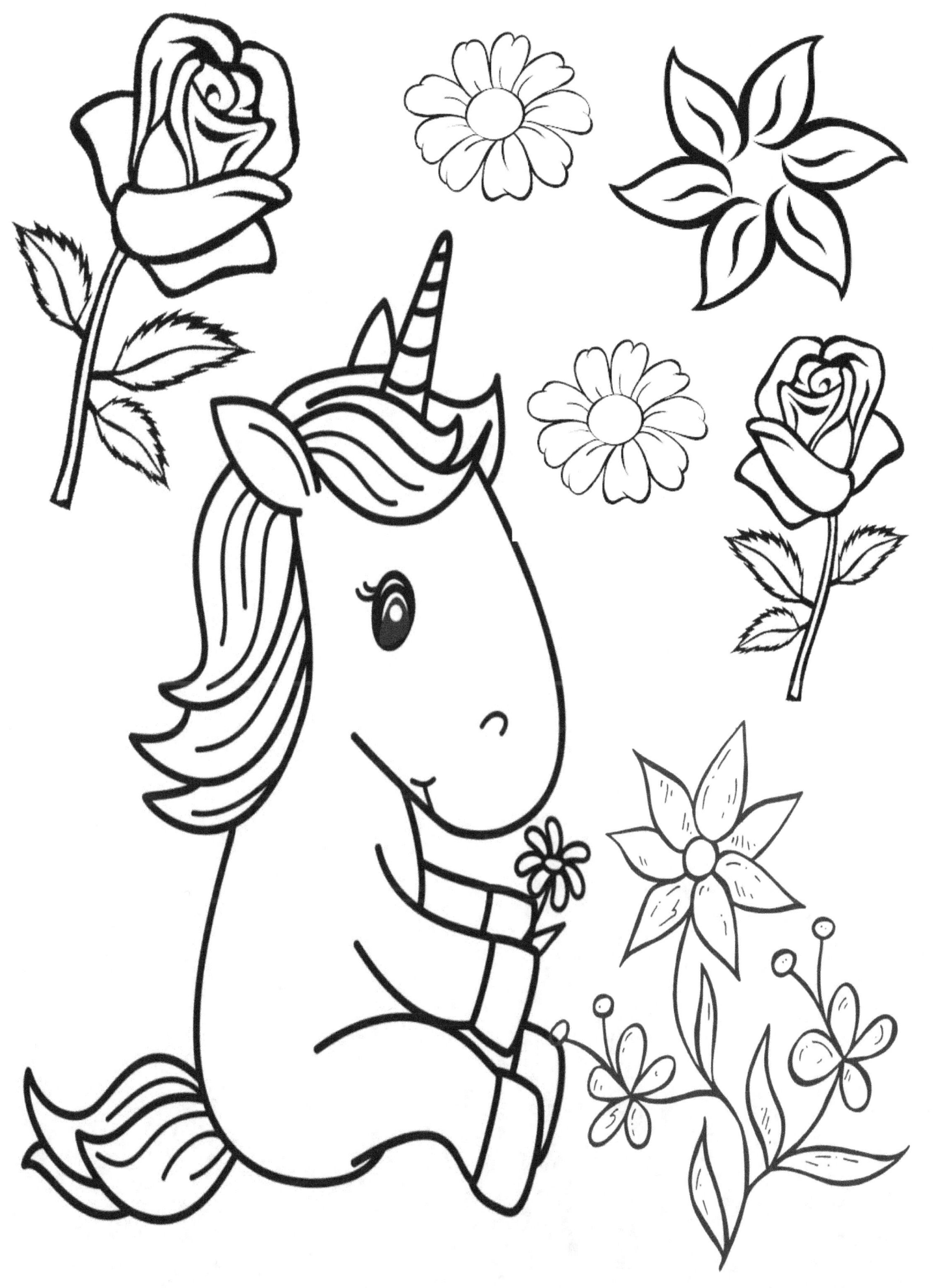

UNICORN

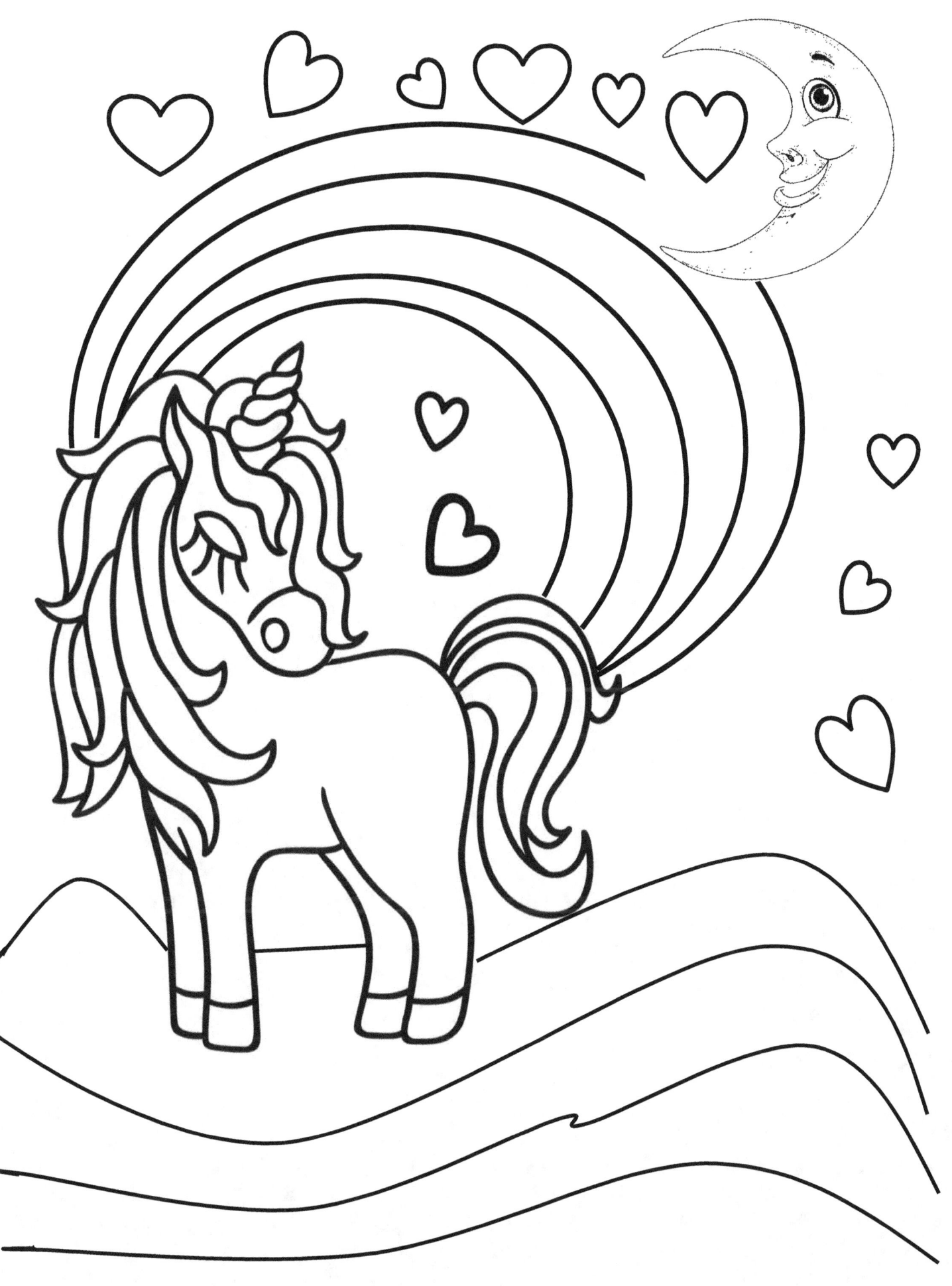

UNICORN

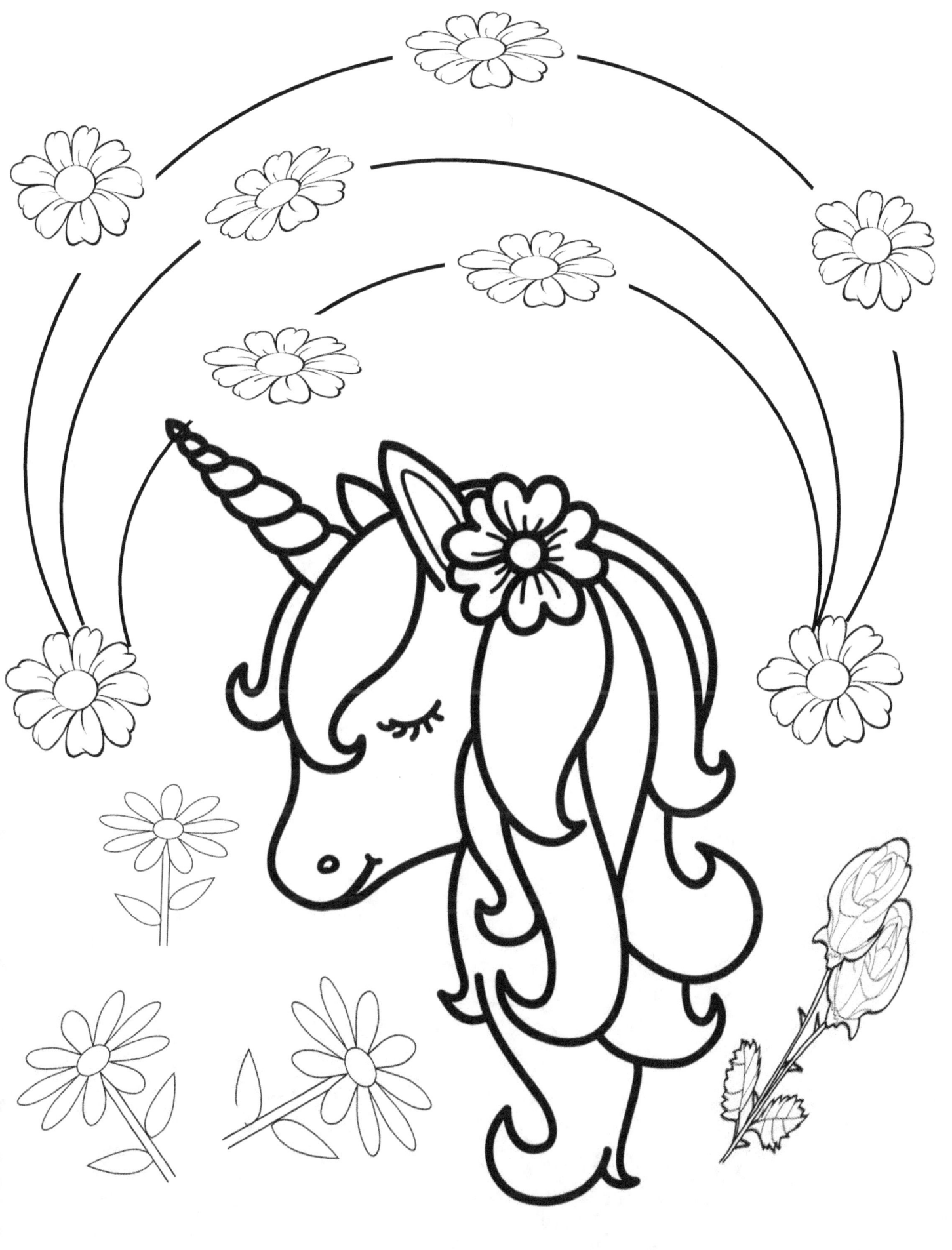

UNICORN

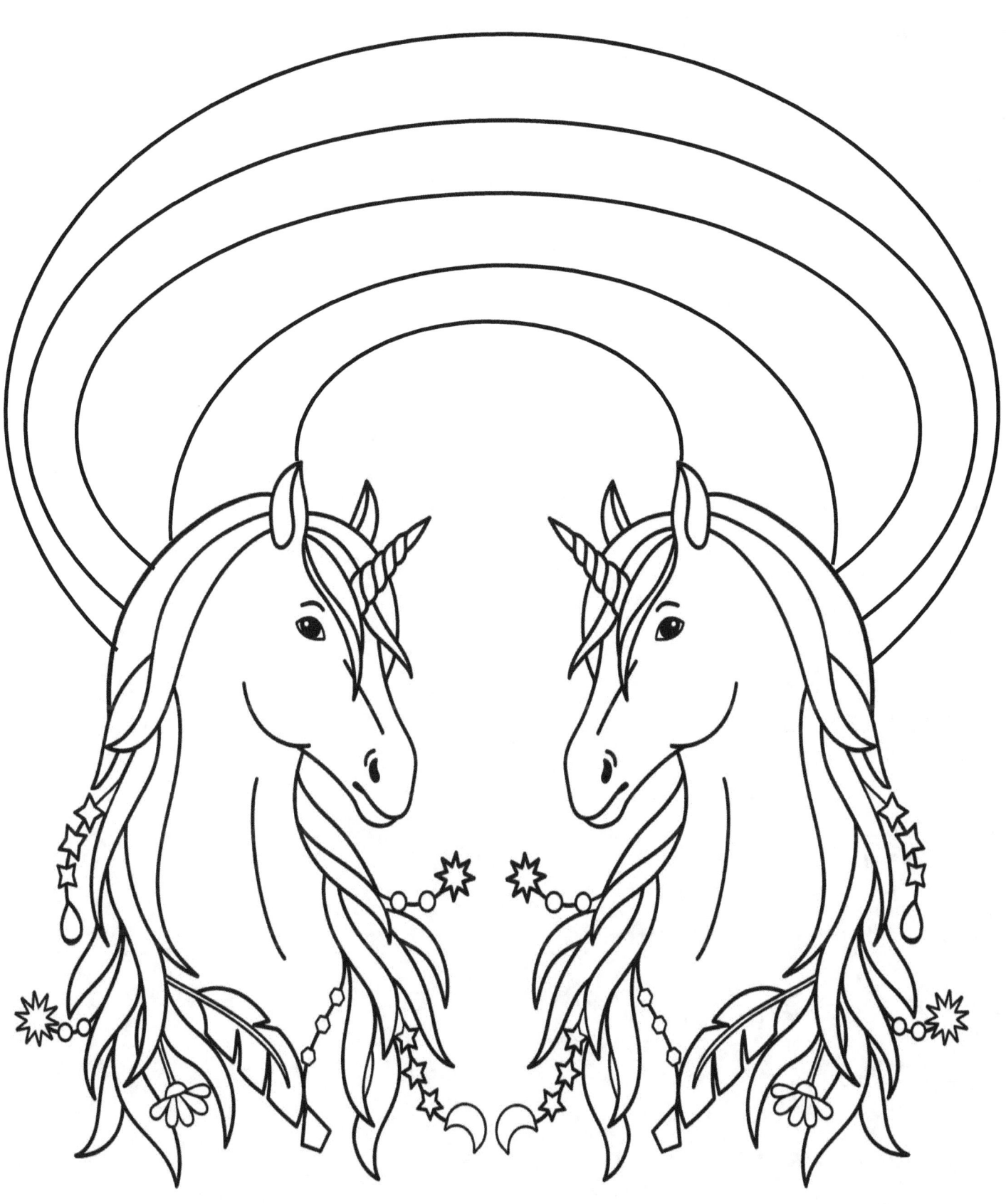

UNICORN

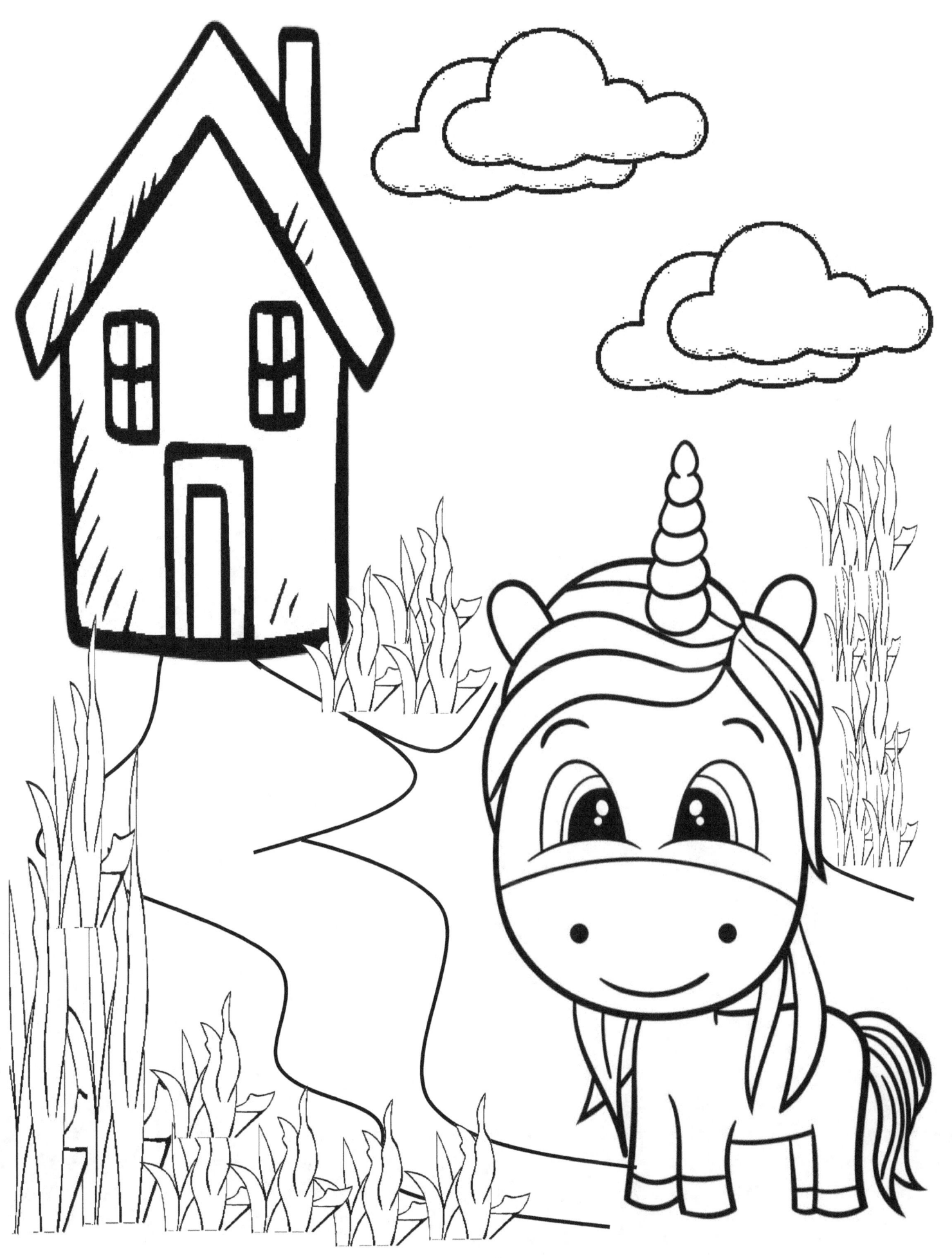

UNICORN

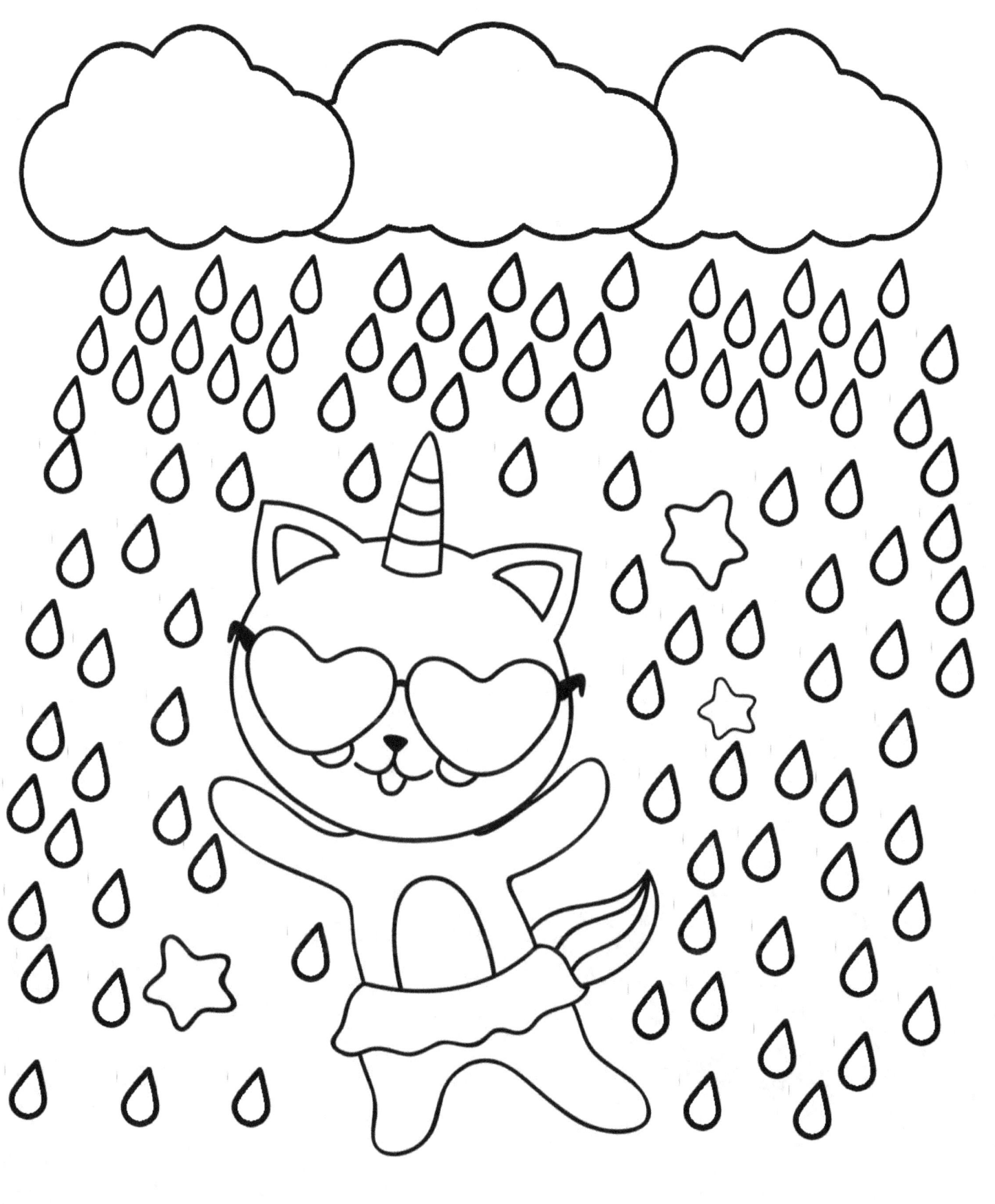

UNICORN

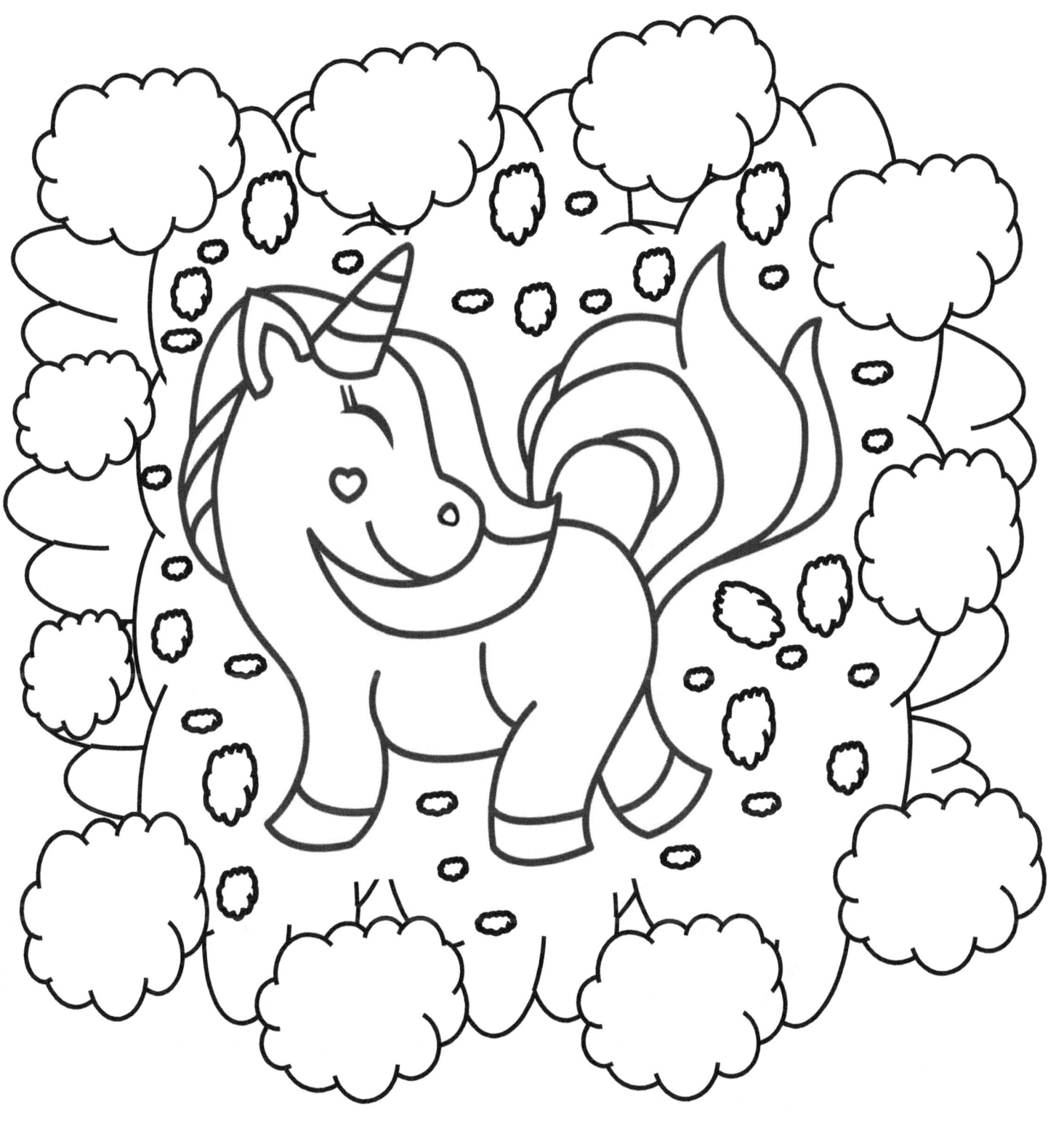

UNICORN

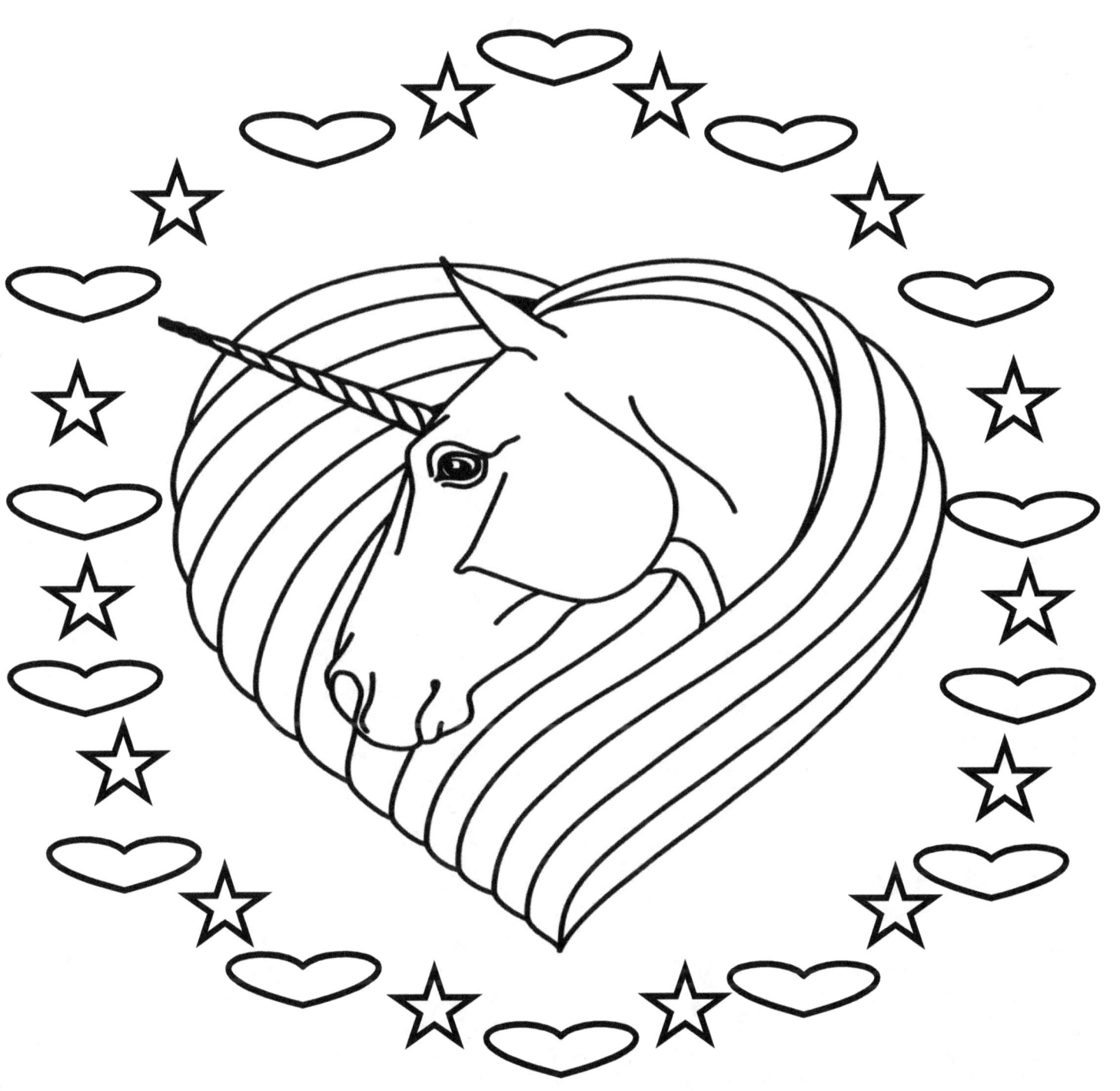

UNICORN

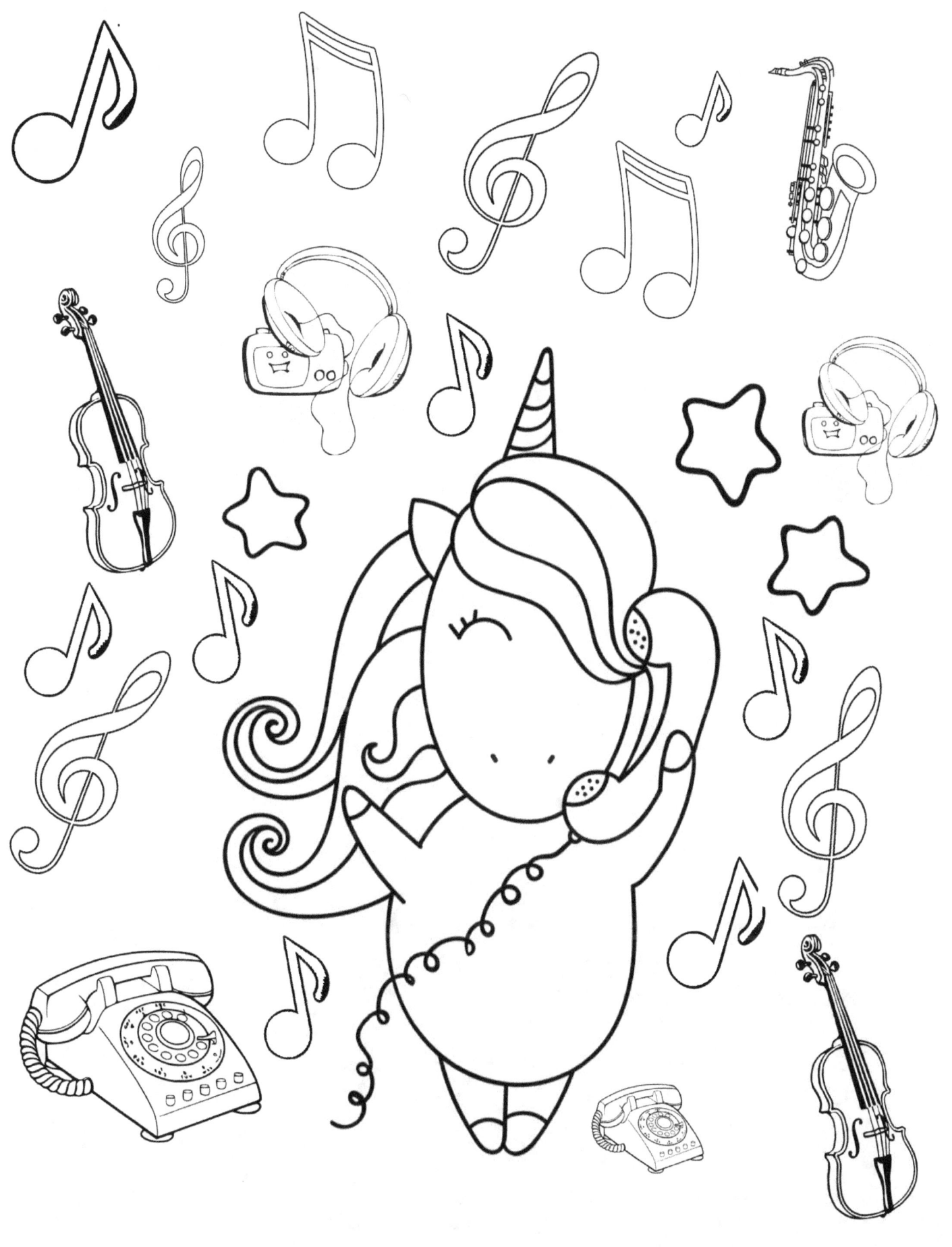

UNICORN

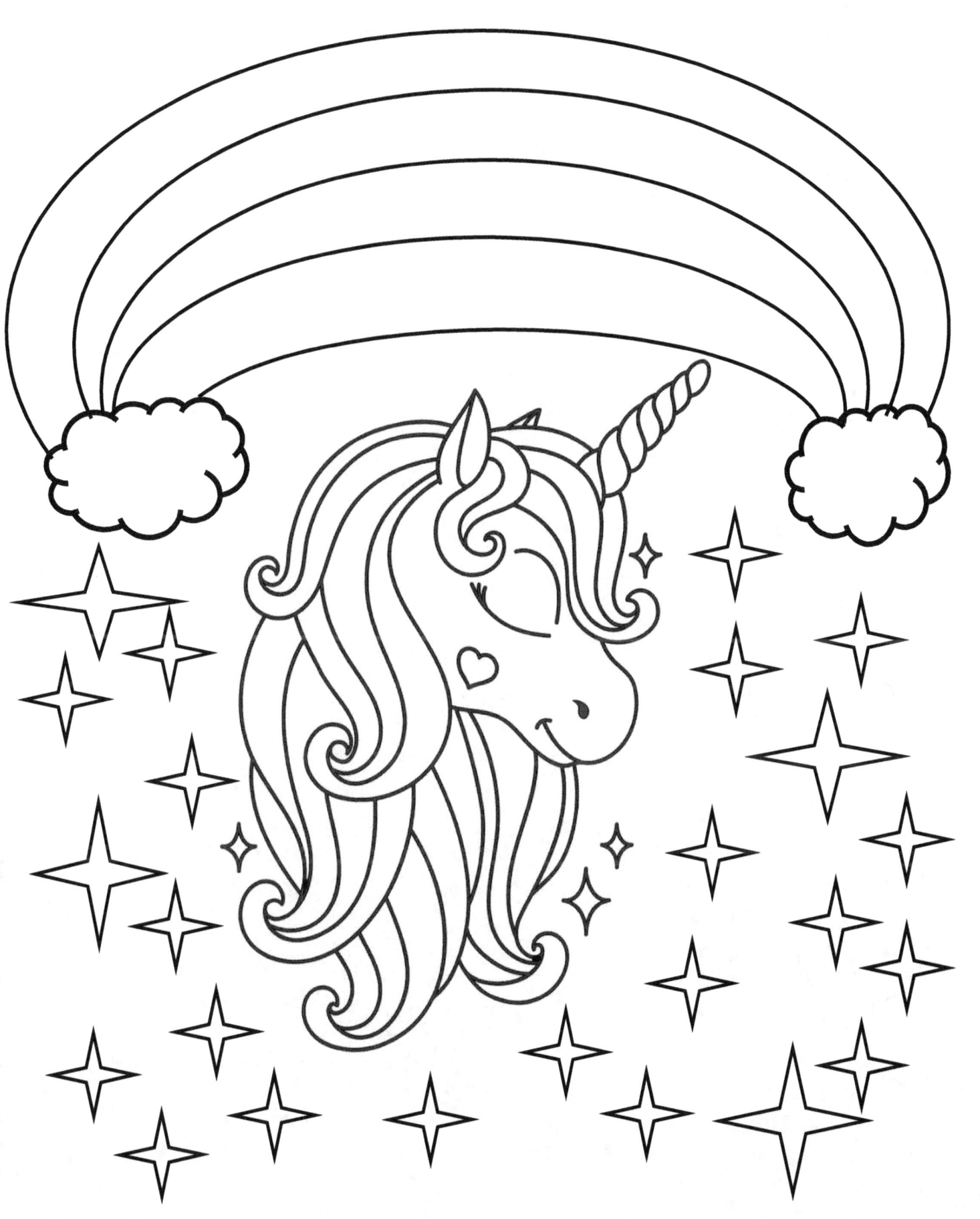

UNICORN

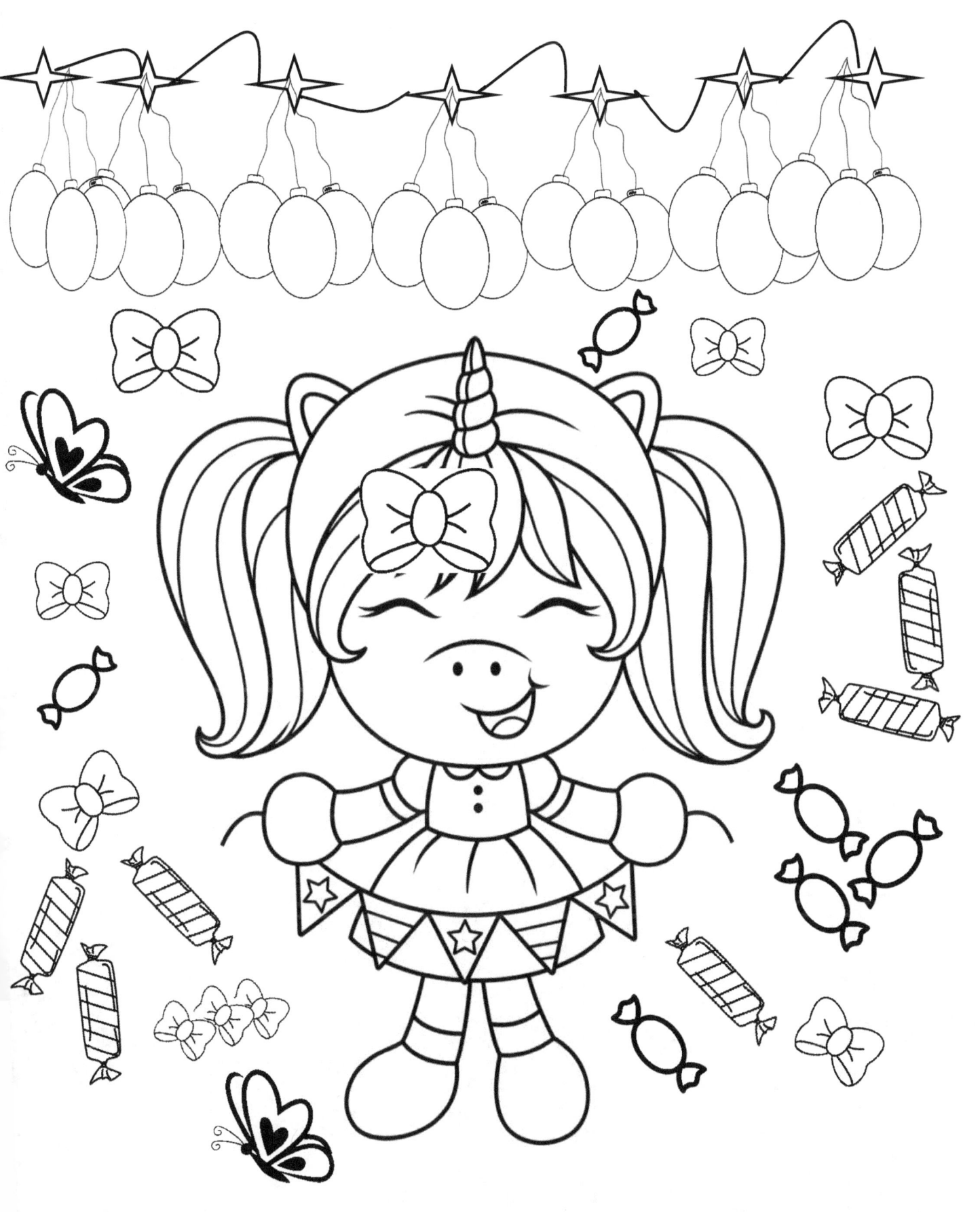

UNICORN

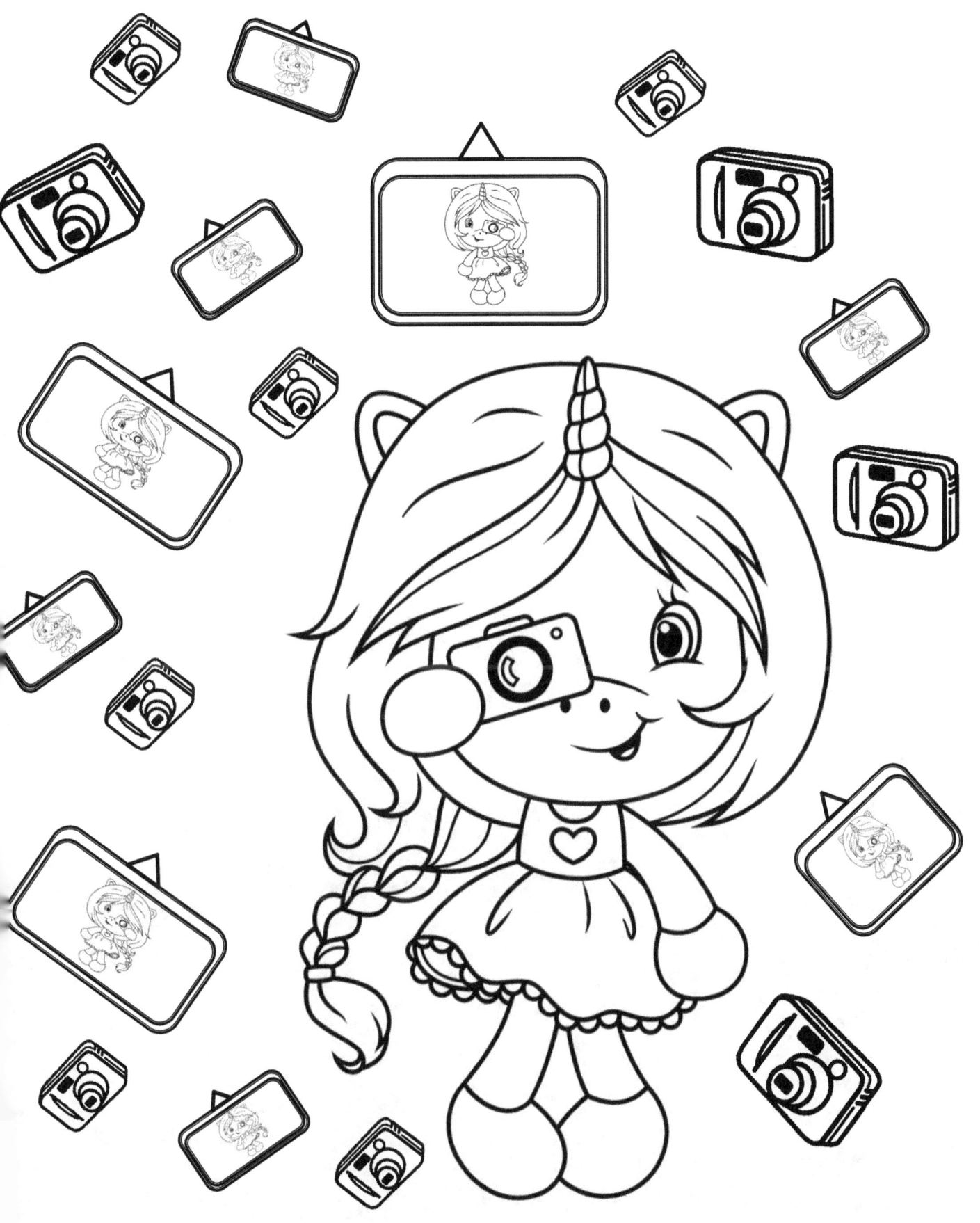

UNICORN

www.ingramcontent.com/pod-product-compliance
Lightning Source LLC
Chambersburg PA
CBHW080508220526
45465CB00006B/2417